mental_floss

EXTRA STRENGTH

Logic Puzzles

Mark Zegarelli

PUZZLE
WRIGHT
PRESS
New York

PUZZLE
WRIGHT
PRESS

New York

An Imprint of Sterling Publishing
1166 Avenue of the Americas
New York, NY 10036

ISBN 978-1-4549-1245-3

Distributed in Canada by Sterling Publishing
c/o Canadian Manda Group, 664 Annette Street
Toronto, Ontario, Canada M6S 2C8
Distributed in the United Kingdom by GMC Distribution Services
Castle Place, 166 High Street, Lewes, East Sussex, England BN7 1XU
Distributed in Australia by Capricorn Link (Australia) Pty. Ltd.
P.O. Box 704, Windsor, NSW 2756, Australia

For information about custom editions, special sales, and premium and
corporate purchases, please contact Sterling Special Sales at 800-805-5489 or
specialsales@sterlingpublishing.com.

Manufactured in China

4 6 8 10 9 7 5 3

www.puzzlewright.com

CONTENTS

INTRODUCTION

Sometimes you need relief from a headache. But if, like me, you love logic puzzles, sometimes a headache is exactly what you're looking for. The U.S. Marines say "Pain is weakness leaving the body." And the brain, like a muscle, needs good workouts at regular intervals to run at peak efficiency.

The puzzles in this book are designed to stretch and grow your brain like a sequence of properly calibrated exercises. If you are new to logic puzzles (or even if you're not), start at the beginning and move forward through the book. You should find each puzzle a little bit more difficult than the previous one.

You'll probably make your way through the first few puzzles in just a few minutes. Then, as you continue, you'll start to feel the burn. You'll also see the difficulty ratings provided with each puzzle increase, from one star to five stars.

Keep on going when the going gets tough! That brain-ache you may feel as you work through these problems is the weakness of unclear thought exiting your cranium. Along the way, if you find yourself really stuck, I've provided a full explanation of every answer in the back of the book.

Consider yourself a champion if you make it past Puzzle #40, and especially if you keep going all the way to the end. The last few puzzles are among the toughest I've ever created. Some of these may take you days, even weeks, to solve. You wanted a challenge, didn't you?

If you stick with this program, you will emerge ready to think through any situation life hands you, with undreamed-of ease and effectiveness.

Happy solving!

—Mark Zegarelli

1 SNAIL MAIL

With email, texting, and a variety of other ways to electronically connect with people, Kevin hardly receives any mail these days. Last week (Monday through Friday) he received just one piece of mail each day. Can you figure out which day Kevin received each piece of mail?

1   Kevin received the credit card offer earlier in the week than he received the wedding invitation, and he received one of these items on Wednesday.

2   He received the letter from his grandmother exactly two days before receiving the mailer on a political candidate.

3   He didn't receive the book of coupons for a local supermarket on Friday.

	Monday	Tuesday	Wednesday	Thursday	Friday
book of coupons					
credit card offer					
letter from grandmother					
political mailer					
wedding invitation					

day	piece of mail

Solution, page 82

2 UPSTAIRS, DOWNSTAIRS ★

James owns a three-story Edwardian house in San Francisco, which has been subdivided into three apartments on the top, middle, and bottom floors. He rents each to a different family (surnamed Bryant, Geary, and Sanchez), each of whom has a different number of children (from 1 to 3). Can you figure out which family lives on each floor, and how many children each has?

1 The Bryant family lives somewhere above the family with one child.

2 The Sanchez family lives somewhere above the family with three children.

3 The Geary family has more children than the family that lives on the top floor.

	surname	number of children
top floor		
middle floor		
bottom floor		

Solution, page 82

3 BAD MOON RISING ★

Zinnia, an astrology enthusiast, is infamous among her friends for her snap decisions based on signs in the stars. In four consecutive weeks, she made four big changes, in each case based on a different astrological phenomenon (one of which was Venus sextiling Scorpio). Can you figure out the order in which Zinnia made these decisions and the sign that prompted each?

1   Zinnia sold her car sometime before she made a decision because Jupiter went retrograde.

2   She changed apartments at least two weeks before she dumped her boyfriend because she found out that his rising sign was incompatible with hers.

3   She didn't quit her job because Mars entered Aries or because Jupiter went retrograde.

	week 1	week 2	week 3	week 4	incompatible rising signs	Jupiter went retrograde	Mars entered Aries	Venus sextiled Scorpio
changed apartments								
dumped her boyfriend								
quit her job								
sold her car								
incompatible rising signs								
Jupiter went retrograde								
Mars entered Aries								
Venus sextiled Scorpio								

week	decision	astrological phenomenon

Solution, page 82

4 CHICAGO, WYOMING ★

The town of Chicago, Wyoming, is far less bustling than its namesake in Illinois. Nestled in the foothills of the Rocky Mountains, the town has only one principal intersection, where Main Street crosses Route 80. At each of the four corners is a different type of business owned by a different person (including Lance). Can you discover who owns each corner location and the type of business he or she owns?

1 The gas station is located at the southwest corner.

2 Sylvia's business is due north of the restaurant.

3 Tyler owns the supermarket.

4 Kelsey's store is not diagonally opposite the hardware store.

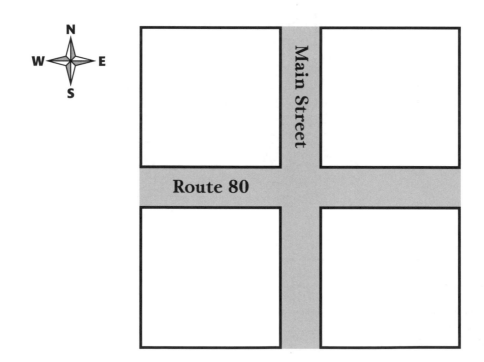

Solution, page 82

5 WORKOUT WARMUPS

Rather than go to the gym, Jacob owns a set of free weights that he uses to work out at his house. His warm-up routine includes four quick sets of exercises (including decline sit-ups), each using one of the four lightest pairs of dumbbells on the rack (including a pair of 20-pound dumbbells). Can you figure out the order in which Jacob does these four warm-up exercises and the set of dumbbells he uses for each?

1 Jacob's fourth exercise uses the 25-pound weights.

2 He does a set of curls immediately before he does a set of military presses.

3 Jacob does a set of bench presses sometime after he uses the 10-pound weights and sometime before he uses the 15-pound weights.

	first exercise	second exercise	third exercise	fourth exercise	10-pound weights	15-pound weights	20-pound weights	25-pound weights
bench presses								
curls								
decline sit-ups								
military presses								
10-pound weights								
15-pound weights								
20-pound weights								
25-pound weights								

order	exercise	weights

Solution, page 82

6 CAN YOU HEAR ME NOW? ★

Gabby is considering changing her cell phone provider. She asked five different friends (including Thomas) for advice, and each recommended his or her current company (including PhonaFriend). Each company provides a different feature to its customers that the other four companies don't offer (one company allows customers to roll over their unused minutes from one month to the next). Can you figure out which friend uses each company, and the feature that this company offers to its customers?

1 James (who doesn't use Telered or WebCon) recommended the company that provides its customers service without committing to a contract.

2 Alex gets his phone service from EarthNet, which doesn't provide its customers free texting or coverage across multiple devices.

3 Hyperion doesn't provide phone service to Faith or James.

4 Telered (which isn't Brianna's provider) is the only company that enables its customers to make calls from anywhere in the world.

5 Faith (who doesn't use Telered) doesn't receive free texting from her company.

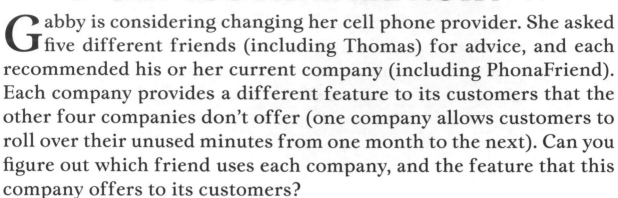

	EarthNet	Hyperion	PhonaFriend	Telered	WebCon	free texting	multiple devices	no contract	rollover minutes	worldwide coverage
Alex										
Brianna										
Faith										
James										
Thomas										
free texting										
multiple devices										
no contract										
rollover minutes										
worldwide coverage										

friend	company	feature

12

Solution, page 82

7 CLASS ACT ★★

For her junior year in high school, Jennifer pushed herself to take eight classes (advanced writing, chemistry, English literature, physics, pre-calculus, statistics, U.S. history, and world geography), which then propelled her to her first-choice university. Can you discover the period (from first to eighth) in which she took each of these classes?

1 Jennifer's statistics class was exactly three periods after her English literature class.

2 Her fourth class was either chemistry or physics.

3 Jennifer took advanced writing during either third or fifth period.

4 Four of Jennifer's eight classes were: physics, U.S. history, her first-period class, and her seventh-period class.

5 She took pre-calculus during either third or eighth period.

6 Jennifer's U.S. history class was earlier in the day than world geography; one of these classes was during sixth period.

	first period	second period	third period	fourth period	fifth period	sixth period	seventh period	eighth period
advanced writing								
chemistry								
English literature								
physics								
pre-calculus								
statistics								
U.S. history								
world geography								

Solution, page 82

8 SPA DAYS ★★

Once a month, Iris treats herself to a day at the spa. On each of her last five visits so far (May through September), she received a different type of body treatment (including Ginger Glow) from a different person. Can you discover the order in which Iris received the five treatments, and who worked with her in each case?

1 During her June visit, Iris received the Herbal Renewal.

2 She received a treatment from Magda exactly three months after she received the Seaweed Wrap.

3 Iris received a treatment from Alexis one month after she received a Body Polish.

4 She received the Javanese Lulur from Talese.

5 She received the treatment from Lizzie sometime before she received the treatment from Shania.

	May	June	July	August	September	Alexis	Lizzie	Magda	Shania	Talese
Body Polish										
Ginger Glow										
Herbal Renewal										
Javanese Lulur										
Seaweed Wrap										
Alexis										
Lizzie										
Magda										
Shania										
Talese										

month	treatment	person

Solution, page 83

9 WHAT'S THE NEWS? ★★

Salamander County has no less than five newspapers, each centered in a different town. Locals tend to rely on each newspaper for a different type of information. Can you match up each newspaper with the town where it's located and the type of news it specializes in?

1 The five newspapers are: the Herald, the Post, the Fayetteville newspaper, the Maple Creek newspaper, and the paper known predominantly for its real estate section.

2 The Tribune is centered in Pottstown.

3 The Ledger's forte isn't its events calendar or its help-wanted section.

4 The Gazette (whose office isn't in Maple Creek) specializes in state politics.

5 The newspaper located in Williamsburg sells either for its help-wanted section or its focus on local gossip.

6 The Post isn't located in Campbell Lake.

	Gazette	Herald	Ledger	Post	Tribune	events calendar	help-wanted section	local gossip	real estate section	state politics
Campbell Lake										
Fayetteville										
Maple Creek										
Pottstown										
Williamsburg										
events calendar					
help-wanted section					
local gossip					
real estate section					
state politics					

city	paper	specialty

10 THE GIFT OF TIME ★★

Tim's collection of offbeat clocks is well-known among his friends. For his last five birthdays (in 2010, 2011, 2012, 2013, and 2014), he received a different type of unusual clock from five different friends. Can you discover who gave Tim a clock for each birthday and the type of clock given?

1 Jeremy gave Tim a clock for his birthday the year before he received a fascinating clock powered by sand falling in a series of hourglasses.

2 Tim received a water clock exactly two years before Elizabeth gave him one of the clocks.

3 Neither Geoffrey nor Wade gave Tim the sundial.

4 Either Geoffrey or Martina gave Tim an outsized version of a spring-powered alarm clock.

5 Tim received the sundial sometime before he received the pendulum clock; he received one of these two clocks in 2011.

6 Either Martina or Wade gave Tim a clock in 2012.

	2010	2011	2012	2013	2014	pendulum	sand-powered	spring-powered	sundial	water
Elizabeth										
Geoffrey										
Jeremy										
Martina										
Wade										
pendulum										
sand-powered										
spring-powered										
sundial										
water										

year	friend	type of clock

Solution, page 83

11 MOTHER'S DAY ARRANGEMENTS ★★

Last Mother's Day, each of Natalie's five children sent her a bouquet of a different type of flower (carnations, gardenias, hydrangeas, roses, and tulips), plus a beautiful floral art piece made from a different material (ceramic, chrome, glass, silk, and wood). Can you figure out who sent each bouquet and art piece?

1 Either Darlene or Eugene sent gardenias.

2 Either Ben or Sean sent a ceramic flower.

3 Eugene sent either the glass or the wood flower.

4 The person who sent roses didn't send a glass flower.

5 Natalie's five children are: Sean, Tamara, the people who sent roses and tulips, and the person who sent a chrome flower.

6 Tamara didn't send a glass flower.

7 Either Ben or Darlene sent silk flowers.

8 The person who sent the wood flower didn't send hydrangeas.

	carnations	gardenias	hydrangeas	roses	tulips	ceramic	chrome	glass	silk	wood
Ben										
Darlene										
Eugene										
Sean										
Tamara										
ceramic										
chrome										
glass										
silk										
wood										

child	bouquet	art material

12 NEW TRADITIONALISM ★★

Sister Isabel is always pleased when her 10th-graders are observant of Catholic traditions. So on Ash Wednesday, she asked her class what they planned to give up for Lent. Six children named forms of technology that didn't even exist when the sister was in school (Amazon Prime, Facebook, Instagram, Netflix, Skype, and Twitter). Can you find the order in which the six children spoke and the form of technology that each plans to give up for Lent?

1 The first two children who spoke plan to give up Instagram and Skype, in some order.

2 Either Matthew or Teresa plans to give up Amazon Prime.

3 Kelly and Patrick spoke, in some order, fourth and fifth.

4 Teresa doesn't plan to give up Skype.

5 One student spoke just after Lloyd and just before the student who plans to give up Netflix.

6 Cathy, who plans to give up Facebook, didn't speak third.

7 Patrick, who doesn't plan to give up Twitter, didn't speak just after Teresa.

	first to speak	second to speak	third to speak	fourth to speak	fifth to speak	sixth to speak	Amazon Prime	Facebook	Instagram	Netflix	Skype	Twitter
Cathy												
Kelly												
Lloyd												
Matthew												
Patrick												
Teresa												
Amazon Prime							
Facebook							
Instagram							
Netflix							
Skype							
Twitter							

order	child	technology

Solution, page 83

13 GARDENING PROJECT ★★

Melinda and Jack, who love gardening, are planning a renovation of their backyard. Each of six sections of the garden (including one area near a brick wall) will feature a different shrub (butterfly bushes, Carolina allspice, hydrangea, oleanders, potentillas, and spireas) and a different perennial flower (ajugas, black-eyed Susans, crocuses, daylilies, poppies, and tulips). See if you can match up each garden area with the shrub and perennial flower that it will feature.

1 The area near the guest house will feature butterfly bushes.

2 One part of the yard will have hydrangea bushes and ajugas.

3 The area near the swimming pool (which will bloom each year with poppies) will not include spireas.

4 The grounds around the treehouse will feature oleanders but not crocuses.

5 The area next to the walkway will include black-eyed susans.

6 The place to be planted with Carolina allspice (which will also have daylilies) isn't the area around the fountain.

	butterfly bushes	Carolina allspice	hydrangeas	oleanders	potentillas	spireas	ajugas	black-eyed Susans	crocuses	daylilies	poppies	tulips
brick wall												
fountain												
guest house												
swimming pool												
treehouse												
walkway												
ajugas												
black-eyed Susans												
crocuses												
daylilies												
poppies												
tulips												

garden section	shrub	flower

14 SCIENCE FAIR ★★

The yearly science fair at Thomas Edison High School is always well-attended; this year, hundreds of students participated, but only six were chosen for distinction: three girls (Bethany, Jennifer, and Miriam) and three boys (Duncan, Evan, and Ralphie). Can you sort out the order in which each of the top six students were ranked and the subject of his or her science project?

1 The three girls are: the student whose topic was magnetism, the student whose topic was projectiles, and the student who won third prize.

2 Ralphie ranked exactly three places above the student whose topic was hybridization.

3 Duncan's project ranked higher than Jennifer's.

4 Bethany's project topic wasn't projectiles.

5 Evan ranked just below the student whose topic was refraction.

6 The fourth prize topic was either earthquakes or magnetism.

7 Miriam's project ranked lower than the project on catalysts.

	first place	second place	third place	fourth place	fifth place	sixth place	catalysts	earthquakes	hybridization	magnetism	projectiles	refraction
Bethany												
Duncan												
Evan												
Jennifer												
Miriam												
Ralphie												
catalysts												
earthquakes												
hybridization												
magnetism												
projectiles												
refraction												

rank	student	subject

20

Solution, page 84*Solution, page 84*

15 SEVEN DEADLY DESSERTS ★★

Jordan has a weekly video blog showcasing her favorite recipes. For the past seven weeks, she's devoted each episode to a different type of chocolate cake named for one of the seven deadly sins. She baked each cake in honor of a different event. Can you link up the week in which Jordan made each cake and the event for which she prepared it?

1 Jordan baked the Chocolate Pride Cake the week before she baked a cake for a housewarming party.

2 She baked the second week's cake for either the baby shower or to celebrate her daughter's getting her driver's license.

3 She baked the Chocolate Lust Cake sometime before she baked the Chocolate Wrath Cake.

4 Jordan baked the Chocolate Sloth Cake either two weeks before or two weeks after she baked the cake for the anniversary party.

5 The fifth cake she baked was either the Chocolate Envy Cake or the Chocolate Lust Cake.

6 Jordan baked the cake for the bon voyage party the week after she baked the cake for the barbecue and the week before she baked the Chocolate Avarice Cake.

7 She baked the Chocolate Gluttony Cake the week after she baked the cake for the baby shower.

8 Jordan baked the sixth cake for either the baby shower or the birthday party.

	first week	second week	third week	fourth week	fifth week	sixth week	seventh week	anniversary	baby shower	barbecue	birthday	bon voyage	driver's license	housewarming
Chocolate Avarice Cake														
Chocolate Envy Cake														
Chocolate Gluttony Cake														
Chocolate Lust Cake														
Chocolate Pride Cake														
Chocolate Sloth Cake														
Chocolate Wrath Cake														
anniversary														
baby shower														
barbecue														
birthday														
bon voyage														
driver's license														
housewarming														

week	cake	event

Solution, page 84

16 CHORE SCHEDULE ★★

Six roommates have agreed that each person will take care of a different weekly chore (cleaning the bathroom, dusting, mopping the kitchen floor, scrubbing the kitchen counters, taking out the trash, vacuuming the carpet). Can you figure out the day (Sunday through Friday) on which each person does his or her chore and the chore in each case?

1 Sophie either cleans the bathroom or scrubs the kitchen counters.

2 On Mondays, one roommate either mops the kitchen floor or vacuums the carpet.

3 Aaron doesn't do his chore the day before Bridget does hers.

4 One roommate does the dusting the day after another roommate takes out the trash and the day before Margot does her chore.

5 Bridget does her chore either the day before or the day after another roommate cleans the bathroom.

6 Either Aaron or Edie vacuums the carpet.

7 George does his chore on Fridays.

	Sunday	Monday	Tuesday	Wednesday	Thursday	Friday	clean bathroom	dust	mop kitchen	scrub counters	take out trash	vacuum carpet
Aaron												
Bridget												
Edie												
George												
Margot												
Sophie												
clean bathroom							
dust							
mop kitchen							
scrub counters							
take out trash							
vacuum carpet							

day	roommate	chore

Solution, page 84

17 RETURN OF THE ALLIGATORS

The Alligators were a band started almost half a century ago by four high school friends (including Eddie). At their 45th high school reunion, the band reformed. Over the course of the night, the band performed four different Beatles songs, each sung by a different person, each of whom played a different instrument. Figure out the order in which the four band members sang the Beatles songs, the song each sang, and the instrument each plays.

1 The first Beatles song that the band performed was either "Lady Madonna" or "Taxman."

2 The bass player sang a Beatles song sometime after "She Loves You" and sometime before Marty sang.

3 Either the guitarist or the pianist sang "Yesterday."

4 Drew sang "Lady Madonna."

5 Randall played either bass or piano.

6 The drummer sang "Taxman."

	first song	second song	third song	fourth song	Drew	Eddie	Marty	Randall	bass	drums	guitar	piano
"Lady Madonna"												
"She Loves You"												
"Taxman"												
"Yesterday"												
bass												
drums												
guitar												
piano												
Drew												
Eddie												
Marty												
Randall												

order	song	singer	instrument

Solution, page 84

18 COEN HEADS ★★

A theater had a 5-night film festival of Coen Brothers movies (from Sunday to Thursday). Each evening, the theater showed two different Coen Brothers movies, an early show and a late show. For each day of the film festival, can you figure out which movies were shown early and late?

1 "No Country for Old Men" and "Raising Arizona" were shown on the same day, in some order.
2 "A Serious Man" and "Fargo" were, in some order, an early show and a late show.
3 The early show on Tuesday was either "Fargo" or "Miller's Crossing."
4 "Blood Simple" was shown on Wednesday.
5 "O Brother, Where Art Thou?" was the early show exactly two days after "The Hudsucker Proxy" was the late show.
6 "The Big Lebowski" was an early show, but not on Monday.
7 The late show on Monday was either "A Serious Man" or "Inside Llewyn Davis."
8 "Blood Simple" and "Inside Llewyn Davis" were, in some order, an early show and a late show.
9 Sunday's movies were in alphabetical order. (Include leading articles when alphabetizing.)

	Sunday, early show	Sunday, late show	Monday, early show	Monday, late show	Tuesday, early show	Tuesday, late show	Wednesday, early show	Wednesday, late show	Thursday, early show	Thursday, late show
"A Serious Man"										
"Blood Simple"										
"Fargo"										
"Inside Llewyn Davis"										
"Miller's Crossing"										
"No Country for Old Men"										
"O Brother, Where Art Thou?"										
"Raising Arizona"										
"The Big Lebowski"										
"The Hudsucker Proxy"										

showing	movie

Solution, page 85

19 RUN FOR YOUR LIFE ★★

The Beachrunners are a running club that meets every morning before work for a group run by the ocean. On Friday, six members were present, each of whom ran a different whole number of miles (three, four, five, six, eight, or ten), from the starting point to a different marker (café, fishing pier, lighthouse, miniature golf course, public pool, or yacht club). Can you figure out how far each person ran, and where each ended his or her run?

1 Patrice ran farther than the person who ran to the lighthouse, and together they ran a total of 14 miles.

2 Roger ran one mile past the fishing pier.

3 Blake ran twice as far as Sara, but not as far as the public pool.

4 The café is two miles past the miniature golf course.

5 Either Donald or Sara ran to the yacht club.

6 Elaine ran either six or eight miles.

	three miles	four miles	five miles	six miles	eight miles	ten miles	café	fishing pier	lighthouse	mini golf course	public pool	yacht club
Blake												
Donald												
Elaine												
Patrice												
Roger												
Sara												
café												
fishing pier												
lighthouse												
mini golf course												
public pool												
yacht club												

distance	runner	marker

20 ERROL'S ERRANDS ★★★

As a personal assistant, Errol is used to running errands for his boss. Yesterday, he ran seven errands on six different streets. Discover the order in which Errol did these errands and the street where each place of business was located.

1 The dry cleaners and the pharmacy are next door to each other on the same street, so Errol dropped off some dry cleaning and picked up a prescription consecutively, though not necessarily in that order.

2 Returning a damaged toaster for a refund was the third errand that Errol did after paying a late electric bill.

3 Errol mailed a package on either Third Avenue or Wendell Way.

	first errand	second errand	third errand	fourth errand	fifth errand	sixth errand	seventh errand	Grandview Terrace	Hyacinth Boulevard	Mulberry Street	Third Avenue	Union Avenue	Wendell Way
bought a gift card													
bought fruit													
dropped off dry cleaning													
mailed a package													
paid the electric bill													
picked up a prescription													
returned a damaged toaster													
Grandview Terrace													
Hyacinth Boulevard													
Mulberry Street													
Third Avenue													
Union Avenue													
Wendell Way													

4 He bought a gift card sometime before running at least one errand on Hyacinth Boulevard.

5 The errand Errol performed just after dropping off the dry cleaning was not on Grandview Terrace.

6 His third errand wasn't on Grandview Terrace or Third Avenue.

7 He bought fruit immediately after running an errand on Union Avenue.

8 Errol's second errand was his only stop on Mulberry Street.

9 His sixth errand was either buying a gift card or mailing a package.

order	errand	street

26

Solution, page 85

21 TAROT INSPIRATION ★★★

Drake uses tarot cards for daily inspiration. Each day last week (Sunday to Saturday), he chose a different major arcana card (Chariot, Fool, Hierophant, Moon, Star, Tower, or Wheel) and a different court card (King or Prince of Swords, Queen or Princess of Pentacles, Queen or Prince of Wands, or Princess of Cups) to help him guide his actions. Can you figure out the two cards that Drake picked each day?

1. Drake chose the Princess of Cups the day after he chose the Prince of Wands and the day before he chose the Wheel.
2. He didn't choose the Moon exactly three days after he chose the Prince of Swords.
3. He chose the Tower on either Wednesday or Friday.
4. On Tuesday and Wednesday, Drake chose the Queen of Pentacles and the Prince of Swords, not necessarily in that order.
5. He chose the Star the day before he chose the Fool.

	Sunday	Monday	Tuesday	Wednesday	Thursday	Friday	Saturday	King of Swords	Queen of Pentacles	Queen of Wands	Prince of Swords	Prince of Wands	Princess of Cups	Princess of Pentacles
The Chariot														
The Fool														
The Hierophant														
The Moon														
The Star														
The Tower														
The Wheel														
King of Swords														
Queen of Pentacles														
Queen of Wands														
Prince of Swords														
Prince of Wands														
Princess of Cups														
Princess of Pentacles														

6. Drake chose the Hierophant two days before he chose the Princess of Pentacles.
7. He chose the King of Swords the day after he chose the Chariot and the day before he chose the Queen of Wands.

day	major arcana card	court card

22 MEETING UP ★★★

Having recently moved to New York City, Andrea is dedicating herself to meeting new friends. Every night this week after work (Monday through Friday), she has attended a different meet-up at a different café. At each event, she met a different person. Can you figure out the day on which Andrea met each person, the café where they met, and the topic of the meet-up?

1 On Monday, Sandra went to a meet-up for Portuguese speakers.

2 She attended the meet-up at Joe to Go no more than two days before she went to the one for bridge players.

3 She met Joyce or Tony at a meet-up for knitting enthusiasts.

4 Sandra met Raoul sometime after she went to the meet-up for cat lovers and sometime before she went to Café Caffeine.

5 She met Joyce the day after she met Leo.

6 She didn't meet Cassius at either Joe to Go or the King of Cups.

7 The meet-up for amateur photographers was at Jumpin' Java.

8 On Friday, she attended a meet-up at Bean and Nothingness.

	Monday	Tuesday	Wednesday	Thursday	Friday	Cassius	Joyce	Leo	Raoul	Tony	amateur photographers	bridge players	cat lovers	knitting enthusiasts	Portuguese speakers
Bean and Nothingness															
Café Caffeine															
Joe to Go															
Jumpin' Java															
King of Cups															
amateur photographers															
bridge players															
cat lovers															
knitting enthusiasts															
Portuguese speakers															
Cassius															
Joyce															
Leo															
Raoul															
Tony															

day	café	person met	meet-up topic

23 BINGE-WATCHING ★★★

Seymour got a 60-inch HDTV for his birthday in December, and since then has been on a binge-watching spree. In each of the eight following months (January through August), he watched every episode of eight different TV series. Fortunately, this hasn't been a solitary occupation: In each case, he watched the show with a different friend. Can you find the person with whom Seymour binge-watched in each month, and the series they watched in each case?

1   Seymour watched "Breaking Bad" either the month before or the month after he watched a show with Patrick.

2   He watched "Game of Thrones" the month after watching a show with Lillian and two months before watching a show with Trevor.

3   He watched "Homeland" with either Augie or Keith.

4   In February and July, Seymour watched "House of Cards" and "Mad Men," in some order.

5   He watched shows with Jeremy and Rhonda in consecutive months, in some order.

6   Seymour didn't watch "Dexter" with Keith or Wanda.

7   He didn't watch "True Blood" with Rhonda.

8   During three consecutive months, he watched "Californication," "Homeland," and "True Blood," in some order; Lillian didn't watch any of those three shows.

9   The month after watching "Mad Men," Seymour didn't watch a show with either Rhonda or Wanda.

	January	February	March	April	May	June	July	August	Augie	Jeremy	Keith	Lillian	Patrick	Rhonda	Trevor	Wanda
"Breaking Bad"																
"Californication"																
"Dexter"																
"Game of Thrones"																
"Homeland"																
"House of Cards"																
"Mad Men"																
"True Blood"																
Augie																
Jeremy																
Keith																
Lillian																
Patrick																
Rhonda																
Trevor																
Wanda																

month	friend	TV series

24 BETTER LATTE THAN NEVER ★★★

Café Zamora is known more for its coffee than for its service. Today, six patrons—three men (Arnold, Eugene, and Jimmy) and three women (Felicia, Hope, and Pandora)—ordered six different types of coffee, but the barista didn't do a very good job of giving everyone the correct drinks. See if you can figure out each person's full name, the drink each ordered, and the drink each received.

1   No one received the item that he or she ordered.

2   Jimmy ordered the decaf latte, but a woman received it.

3   Arnold is surnamed either Reeves or Valentino.

4   Felicia ordered either the French-pressed coffee or the macchiato.

5   Hope and the person surnamed Banks received the items that each other ordered.

6   Valentino didn't receive the macchiato.

7   Reeves ordered either the café Borgia or the French-pressed coffee.

8   Eugene received the item that DuBois ordered, and Thompson received the item that Eugene ordered.

9   Schumacher received either the café Borgia or the double espresso.

10 Pandora either ordered or received the depth charge.

	Banks	DuBois	Reeves	Schumacher	Thompson	Valentino	ordered café Borgia	ordered decaf latte	ordered depth charge	ordered double espresso	ordered French press	ordered macchiato	received café Borgia	received decaf latte	received depth charge	received double espresso	received French press	received macchiato
Arnold																		
Eugene																		
Felicia																		
Hope																		
Jimmy																		
Pandora																		
received café Borgia																		
received decaf latte																		
received depth charge																		
received double espresso																		
received French press																		
received macchiato																		
ordered café Borgia																		
ordered decaf latte																		
ordered depth charge																		
ordered double espresso																		
ordered French press																		
ordered macchiato																		

first name	last name	drink ordered	drink received

Solution, page 86

25 COSTUME PARTY ★★★

The day before Halloween, Janey had a Halloween party at her house, and invited eight friends from school, who included four boys (Bryan, Eric, Jack, and Victor) and four girls (Angela, Iris, Maria, and Wendy). Each of the eight children wore a costume. Can you figure out the order in which the eight children arrived at the party, and the costume that each wore?

1 Two of the boys' costumes were Spider-Man and Batman, while two of the girls' costumes were a princess and a witch.

2 Jack didn't dress as a robot.

3 Either Bryan or Victor arrived third.

4 Iris arrived just before the child who wore the clown costume.

5 The child who dressed as a ghost arrived just after Eric and just before the child who dressed as a princess.

6 Angela arrived just after the child who wore the Batman costume.

7 The child who dressed as a witch arrived either first or fourth.

8 Maria arrived sometime before Wendy.

9 The last two children to arrive at the party were both boys.

10 The child who dressed as Spider-Man arrived just before the child who dressed as a robot.

11 Victor (who didn't dress as a vampire) wasn't the last child to arrive at the party.

	first	second	third	fourth	fifth	sixth	seventh	eighth	Batman	clown	ghost	princess	robot	Spider-Man	vampire	witch
Angela																
Bryan																
Eric																
Iris																
Jack																
Maria																
Victor																
Wendy																
Batman																
clown																
ghost																
princess																
robot																
Spider-Man																
vampire																
witch																

order	child	costume

26 PEANUT BETTER SANDWICHES ★★★

Every school day, Josh brown-bags a lunch consisting of a sandwich that contains peanut butter and a variety of other items not normally associated with that sticky spread. Last week, from Monday through Friday, he made five different sandwiches, each containing peanut butter and two additional items. Can you sort out which two items Josh added to his peanut butter sandwich on each day?

	Monday	Tuesday	Wednesday	Thursday	Friday
anchovies					
bacon					
olives					
peaches					
pesto					
pickles					
raisins					
sardines					
tartar sauce					
whitefish					

1 On one day, Josh made his specialty sandwich, which includes bacon and peaches.

2 He made the sandwich with pickles exactly three days before he made the sandwich with whitefish.

3 Josh didn't mix olives with raisins.

4 He didn't mix anchovies with whitefish.

5 He used sardines on a sandwich exactly two days before he used tartar sauce.

6 He added pesto to his sandwich on either Tuesday or Friday.

7 Josh made the sandwich with olives exactly three days before he made the sandwich with anchovies.

day	ingredients

Solution, page 87

27 PETTING ZOO ★★★

Eight children from a home-schooling group visited a petting zoo, where they could interact with eight different types of animals (including goats). Of those animals, each child liked a different type best. Using the map below, can you figure out the location of each type of animal's pen, and which child liked each animal best?

1 Juan's favorite type of animal is housed south of the path.

2 Zach liked the pigs best.

3 The three animals housed in pens #2, #4, and #7 are, in some order, ducks, rabbits, and sheep.

4 Emily's favorite type of animal lives in pen #3 or pen #4.

5 The donkeys and the sheep are housed either next to each other or directly across the path from each other.

6 The chickens are housed in the pen directly north of the pen where Simon's favorite type of animal is kept.

7 Kate, William, and Zach chose, in some order, the animals housed in pens #2, #5, and #8 as their favorite animals.

8 Martin's favorite type of animal is housed in the pen directly across the path from where the rabbits live.

9 Alison's favorite type of animal lives in the pen directly across from where William's favorite type of animal lives.

10 Kate's favorite type of animal is housed on the same side of the path as the llamas.

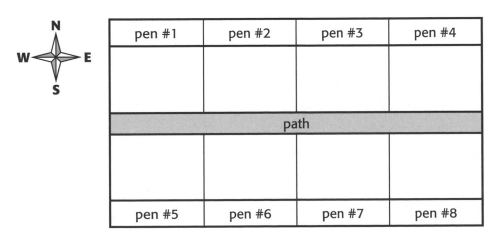

28 DOG DAYS ★★★

Although Abby adores dogs, the apartment where she lives strictly forbids her to own one. As a result, she makes a special point of visiting frequently with friends who own dogs. Last week, on five different days (Monday through Friday), she visited with a different friend every day, each of whom owns a dog (including Cha-Cha) of a distinct breed (including a beagle). Can you discover the day on which Abby visited each friend, the name of each person's dog, and its breed?

1 Abby visited the person who owns Spunky sometime after visiting Wayne and sometime before visiting the person with the sheepdog.

2 She visited Miguel sometime before she visited the person who owns the cocker spaniel.

3 She visited Jordan either the day before or the day after she visited Pepper's owner.

4 Abby visited Susan three days before she visited the person who owns the dachshund.

5 She visited the owner of the Yorkshire terrier sometime before she visited Falafel's owner.

6 Vicki owns the dog named Baby.

7 On Tuesday, Abby visited either Jordan or Miguel.

	Monday	Tuesday	Wednesday	Thursday	Friday	Baby	Cha-Cha	Falafel	Pepper	Spunky	beagle	cocker spaniel	dachshund	sheepdog	Yorkshire terrier
Jordan															
Miguel															
Susan															
Vicki															
Wayne															
beagle															
cocker spaniel															
dachshund															
sheepdog															
Yorkshire terrier															
Baby															
Cha-Cha															
Falafel															
Pepper															
Spunky															

day	friend	dog's name	dog's breed

29 KEYS TO REBECCA ★★★

Rebecca thrives on organization. Even her key ring is rigorously organized, with every one (attic, basement, front door, garage, in-laws' apartment, office, and storage room) a different color and placed in a set order, counting from her distinctive computer chip car key. Can you discover the order in which Rebecca keeps her seven keys on her ring and the color of each?

1   The first key on the ring doesn't open the front door to Rebecca's house.

2   The second key on the ring is either gold or purple.

3   The attic key is next to the blue key.

4   The storage room key is directly between the red and silver keys.

5   The seven keys are: the keys to the garage, the in-laws' apartment, and the storage room; the blue, red, and white keys; and the sixth key on the ring.

6   The silver key opens either the attic or the basement.

7   The garage key is either third or fourth on the ring.

8   The yellow key is directly between the key to the office and the gold key.

	first	second	third	fourth	fifth	sixth	seventh	blue	gold	purple	red	silver	white	yellow
attic														
basement														
front door														
garage														
in-laws' apartment														
office														
storage room														
blue														
gold														
purple														
red														
silver														
white														
yellow														

order	key	color

30 ROLL PLAY ★★★

Once a year, Oliver used to take his jar of coins to a counting machine and willingly paid a percentage of its worth to receive paper money in exchange. But now, he's found a way to save the money—his grandchildren. Like most children, all four of his grandchildren love to count and roll coins. He set each child to the task of counting and wrapping a different valuation of coin, then brought the completed rolls of coins to the bank. Can you figure out each child's age, the denomination of coin that he or she wrapped, and the number of rolls each completed?

1 Lydia, who wrapped 9 rolls of coins, is two years younger than one of the other children.

2 Stephen's age in years isn't the same as the number of rolls of coins that he wrapped.

3 The child who wrapped dimes is 10 years old.

4 The child who wrapped 11 rolls of coins is an odd number of years old.

5 At the end of the day, there were either three or four more rolls of nickels than there were of another denomination of coin.

6 The child who wrapped an even number of rolls of quarters is a year older than one of the other children.

7 Todd, who is 8 years old, wrapped either pennies or nickels.

8 Melanie wrapped exactly one fewer roll of coins than one of the other children.

9 At the end of the day, there were more rolls of pennies than any other denomination of coin.

	age __	age __	age __	age __	__ rolls of coins	__ rolls of coins	__ rolls of coins	__ rolls of coins	pennies	nickels	dimes	quarters
Lydia												
Melanie												
Stephen												
Todd												
pennies												
nickels												
dimes												
quarters												
__ rolls of coins												
__ rolls of coins												
__ rolls of coins												
__ rolls of coins												

child	age	number of rolls	coin

31 SLAMMING POETRY ★★★

Six people (including Blake) read original poems (including "Lost and Not Found") at a poetry slam, in each case punctuating his or her poem with a different odd theatrical gesture not usually found in poetry (one poet read while repeatedly beating his or her chest). Can you figure out the order in which the six poets read their work, the poem each read, and what each did as he or she was reading?

1 The first poet to read punctuated his or her poem with a sequence of loud, piercing screams.

2 Tamarynd read "Grace Under Pressure" while banging her head with a rubber mallet.

3 Mary Jo read sometime after the poet who hopped around on one foot while reading a poem, and sometime before the poet who read "Blissful Remembrance."

4 Victor read his poem sometime after the person who read while stumbling around the stage with a blindfold.

5 Claire didn't read "Blissful Remembrance" or "Naturally, I'm Chagrined."

6 Arlo read his poem third.

7 The author of "Fingers on the Blackboard" read while cracking eggs over his or her head.

8 "Kittens and Puppies" was the sixth poem to be read.

	first	second	third	fourth	fifth	sixth	"Blissful Remembrance"	"Fingers on the Blackboard"	"Grace Under Pressure"	"Kittens and Puppies"	"Lost and Not Found"	"Naturally, I'm Chagrined"	banged head with mallet	cracked eggs over head	hopped on one foot	punctuated poem with screams	repeatedly beat chest	stumbled around blindfolded
Arlo																		
Blake																		
Claire																		
Mary Jo																		
Tamarynd																		
Victor																		
banged head with mallet																		
cracked eggs over head																		
hopped on one foot																		
punctuated poem with screams																		
repeatedly beat chest																		
stumbled around blindfolded																		
"Blissful Remembrance"													
"Fingers on the Blackboard"													
"Grace Under Pressure"													
"Kittens and Puppies"													
"Lost and Not Found"													
"Naturally, I'm Chagrined"													

order	poet	poem	theatrical gesture

32 LIT UP ★★★

In eight different consecutive months (from September 2013 to April 2014), Georgia published a different short story in a different literary magazine. Can you figure out the month in which Georgia published each story and where she published it?

1 "My Side" was published in either November 2013 or January 2014.

2 "If You Want to Know the Truth ..." was published in either 27 Letters or Neverending Stories.

3 "Better Cheer Up" was published two months after the story published in Word Up and two months before the story published in Athena Magazine.

4 "Vigilant Love" was published sometime after the story that was published in Neverending Stories.

5 "Three-Legged Stool Pigeon" was published the month after the story that appeared in South Carolina Quarterly.

6 Golden Gate Gazette didn't publish Georgia's story in December 2013.

7 "Have You Got an Umbrella?" wasn't published in Post-Punk Playbook.

8 "Left to Your Own Devices" and the story that appeared in Neverending Stories were published in different years.

9 Georgia's eight stories are: "A Cross to Bear," "Have You Got an Umbrella?," and "Vigilant Love"; the three stories published in Athena Magazine, Rhode Island Review, and Word Up; and the two stories published in October 2013 and March 2014.

	September 2013	October 2013	November 2013	December 2013	January 2014	February 2014	March 2014	April 2014	27 Letters	Athena Magazine	Golden Gate Gazette	Neverending Stories	Post-Punk Playbook	Rhode Island Review	South Carolina Quarterly	Word Up
"A Cross to Bear"																
"Better Cheer Up"																
"Have You Got an Umbrella?"																
"If You Want to Know the Truth …"																
"Left to Your Own Devices"																
"My Side"																
"Three-Legged Stool Pigeon"																
"Vigilant Love"																
27 Letters																
Athena Magazine																
Golden Gate Gazette																
Neverending Stories																
Post-Punk Playbook																
Rhode Island Review																
South Carolina Quarterly																
Word Up																

month	short story	literary magazine

Solution, page 88

33 CHILI TODAY ★★★★

Lollapalooza County held its annual Chili Cook-off last week to a record crowd. The top six winners (including Lorraine) all received prizes and a chance to compete in the statewide competition. Each winning contestant credited his or her success to the presence of a different secret ingredient not commonly found in chili (blueberry preserves, grapefruit juice, lima beans, sauerkraut, vermouth, and white chocolate). Can you figure out the order of the top six winners, each person's full name, and his or her secret ingredient?

1 McNeill's chili ranked just behind the chili whose secret ingredient was grapefruit juice.

2 Sarah's chili, which includes either blueberry preserves or vermouth, was ranked someplace behind Dakins's chili.

3 Scholler and the contestant whose chili includes white chocolate are, in some order, the contestant whose chili ranked second and the person whose chili ranked two places ahead of Kathleen's chili.

4 Watkins's chili includes neither blueberry preserves nor grapefruit juice.

5 Andrew's chili ranked someplace ahead of Scholler's chili.

6 Either Phelps or Watkins includes white chocolate as a secret ingredient.

7 The chili whose secret ingredient was sauerkraut ranked just behind the chili whose secret ingredient was lima beans.

8 Nick isn't surnamed Scholler or Zenakis.

9 Geoffrey's chili includes either sauerkraut or vermouth.

10 The six winners were: Andrew, Dakins, the person whose chili includes lima beans, the fourth-place winner, the person whose chili ranked just ahead of Sarah, and the person whose chili ranked just behind McNeill.

	first place	second place	third place	fourth place	fifth place	sixth place	Dakins	McNeill	Phelps	Scholler	Watkins	Zenakis	blueberry preserves	grapefruit juice	lima beans	sauerkraut	vermouth	white chocolate
Andrew																		
Geoffrey																		
Kathleen																		
Lorraine																		
Nick																		
Sarah																		
blueberry preserves																		
grapefruit juice																		
lima beans																		
sauerkraut																		
vermouth																		
white chocolate																		
Dakins																		
McNeill																		
Phelps																		
Scholler																		
Watkins																		
Zenakis																		

place	first name	last name	secret ingredient

34 DAILY BREAD ★★★★

Jill and Marlon run a small but successful home bakery. Their specialty is bread loaves. They filled orders for six different types of bread, in each case making a different number of loaves (15, 20, 25, 30, 35, or 40) for a different event. Can you figure out the order in which they filled the six bread orders and the number of loaves they made in each case?

1   The order for the conference was filled sometime after the order for Irish soda bread and sometime before the order for 40 loaves.

2   The order for Jewish rye was for 15 more loaves than the second order that Jill and Marlon filled.

3   They filled the order for the graduation sometime before filling the order for Granary bread.

4   The first four bread orders were, in some order: the orders for ciabatta and Granary bread and the orders for 20 and 30 loaves.

5   The pumpernickel order was for either the conference or the farewell party.

6   They filled the order for the camping trip sometime after they filled the order for French baguettes.

7   The order for 15 loaves of bread, which wasn't for ciabatta, was either the third or fourth order that Jill and Marlon filled.

8   They filled the order for the wedding either just before or just after filling the order for Jewish rye.

9   The fifth order that Jill and Marlon filled contained more loaves than the order for the picnic and fewer loaves than the order for Irish soda bread.

10 The order for the graduation was for more loaves than the order for the farewell party.

	first	second	third	fourth	fifth	sixth	15 loaves	20 loaves	25 loaves	30 loaves	35 loaves	40 loaves	ciabatta	French baguettes	Granary bread	Irish soda bread	Jewish rye	pumpernickel
camping trip																		
conference																		
farewell party																		
graduation																		
picnic																		
wedding																		
ciabatta																		
French baguettes																		
Granary bread																		
Irish soda bread																		
Jewish rye																		
pumpernickel																		
15 loaves																		
20 loaves																		
25 loaves																		
30 loaves																		
35 loaves																		
40 loaves																		

order	event	bread	number of loaves

35 LOOKING FOR DIRECTION ★★★★

On a long road trip to her cousin's house, Emma's GPS suddenly died, leaving her directionless. Fortunately, Emma had been there a few times before, so she was able to remember the way, thanks to a series of landmarks along the road. Once she left the interstate, she remembered that there were a total of three left turns and three right turns to get to the house, with each turn heralded by a different landmark. Can you figure out the order in which Emma turned onto each street, the direction she turned onto it, and the landmark that reminded her to turn?

1   Emma's turn onto Bates Road and her second turn after leaving the interstate were in opposite directions.

2   She made the first of her three right turns onto Sullivan Street.

3   Her turn onto Kendall Drive was at either a car wash or a pharmacy.

4   Emma's three left turns were: the turn onto Hollywood Avenue, the turn at the amusement park, and her fifth turn.

5   Her turn onto Piedmont Pike wasn't immediately after her turn at either the car wash or the furniture store.

6   Emma's third turn and her turn at the furniture store were in opposite directions.

7   Her turn at a brightly colored ice cream stand, onto either Piedmont Pike or Villanova Way, was either her third or her sixth turn.

8   Emma's turn at the museum was either her fourth or fifth turn.

9   She turned at the amusement park at least two turns after turning onto Bates Road.

	first turn	second turn	third turn	fourth turn	fifth turn	sixth turn	left turn	right turn	amusement park	car wash	furniture store	ice cream stand	museum	pharmacy
Bates Road														
Hollywood Avenue														
Kendall Drive														
Piedmont Pike														
Sullivan Street														
Villanova Way														
amusement park														
car wash														
furniture store														
ice cream stand														
museum														
pharmacy														
left turn														
right turn														

order	street	direction of turn	landmark

36 COLORFUL KARAOKE ★★★★

Last night, six friends met at a karaoke bar. Each person sang a different song (including "Black Velvet" and "All Cats Are Gray"). By an odd coincidence, each person's surname is a color mentioned in one of the six songs, and each person wore one of these six colors. Can you figure out each person's full name, the song each sang, and the color each wore?

1   For each singer, his or her last name, the color mentioned in his or her song, and the color that each wore are all different.

2   The six people are: Elaine, the person surnamed Brown, the person surnamed White, the person who sang "Atom Tan," the person who wore black, and the person who wore gray.

3   Arnold's last name is in the title of the song that Beverly Gold sang.

4   The person surnamed Gray sang "White Rabbit."

5   Chuck's last name isn't in the title of the song that Frances sang.

6   The six people are: Douglas, the person surnamed Tan, the person who sang "Bad, Bad Leroy Brown," the person who sang "Heart of Gold," the person who wore gray, and the person who wore white.

54

	Black	Brown	Gold	Gray	Tan	White	black clothes	brown clothes	gold clothes	gray clothes	tan clothes	white clothes	"All Cats Are Gray"	"Atom Tan"	"Bad, Bad Leroy Brown"	"Black Velvet"	"Heart of Gold"	"White Rabbit"
Arnold																		
Beverly																		
Chuck																		
Douglas																		
Elaine																		
Frances																		
"All Cats Are Gray"																		
"Atom Tan"																		
"Bad, Bad Leroy Brown"																		
"Black Velvet"																		
"Heart of Gold"																		
"White Rabbit"																		
black clothes																		
brown clothes																		
gold clothes																		
gray clothes																		
tan clothes																		
white clothes																		

first name	last name	song	clothes

37 PUBLIC SPEAKING ★★★★

At a recent public speaking class, five students made presentations. Each speech lasted a different number of minutes (6, 7, 8, 9, or 10) and was on a different topic. In each case, the speaker was working on improving a different aspect of public speaking (one person was working on his or her organization of main points). Can you discover the order in which the five people spoke, his or her topic, what each was working on, and the length of each speech?

1 Ursula used her speech to work on her body language.

2 Four speeches, in chronological order but not necessarily consecutively, were: the 6-minute speech, the speech made by the person who was working on eye contact, Rodney's speech, and the speech about starting a business.

3 The 7-minute speech was about penguins' mating habits.

4 The second speech of the evening was one minute longer than the speech about a family wedding and one minute shorter than Sharon's speech.

5 Victoria's speech was shorter than the one in which the speaker was working on making smooth slideshow presentations.

6 Rodney's speech was longer than the speech about hang gliding.

7 Four speeches, in chronological order but not necessarily consecutively, were: the speech about angels, the speech in which the speaker was working on vocal variety, Tomas's speech, and the 10-minute speech.

8 Tomas gave the 8-minute speech.

	first	second	third	fourth	fifth	6 minutes	7 minutes	8 minutes	9 minutes	10 minutes	body language	eye contact	organization of points	smooth slideshows	vocal variety	angels	family wedding	hang gliding	penguins	starting a business
Rodney																				
Sharon																				
Tomas																				
Ursula																				
Victoria																				
angels																				
family wedding																				
hang gliding																				
penguins																				
starting a business																				
body language																				
eye contact																				
organization of points																				
smooth slideshows																				
vocal variety																				
6 minutes																				
7 minutes																				
8 minutes																				
9 minutes																				
10 minutes																				

order	name	topic	improvement	length

Solution, page 90

38 ABCS OF BUSINESS TRAVEL ★★★★

On six different business trips, Natalie traveled to a different city (Austin, Baltimore, Chicago, Denver, Evanston, and Fargo), where she stayed in a different hotel (Aston International, Best Western, Crowne Plaza, Days Inn, Embassy Suites, Fairfield Inn), and rented a different type of car (Acura, BMW, Chevrolet, Dodge, Edsel, Fiat). Can you match up each city with the hotel where Natalie stayed and the type of car she rented?

1 On each of Natalie's six business trips, the three initials of the city, the hotel where she stayed, and the car that she rented were all different.

2 For fun, Natalie rented a mint-condition Edsel in either Chicago or Fargo, and stayed during that trip at either the Aston International or the Fairfield Inn.

3 When Natalie rented a Fiat, she didn't stay at either the Best Western or the Days Inn.

4 The initial of the city where Natalie rented the Acura is different from the initial of the car she rented when she stayed at the Best Western.

5 Natalie didn't stay at the Best Western in either Denver or Fargo.

6 When Natalie stayed at the Fairfield Inn, she didn't rent a BMW.

7 When she stayed at the Crowne Plaza, which was in either Denver or Evanston, she rented either the Acura or the Dodge.

8 In Fargo, Natalie didn't rent a BMW.

9 In Austin, where Natalie stayed either at the Days Inn or the Embassy Suites, she rented either a Chevrolet or a Fiat.

	Aston International	Best Western	Crowne Plaza	Days Inn	Embassy Suites	Fairfield Inn	Acura	BMW	Chevrolet	Dodge	Edsel	Fiat
Austin												
Baltimore												
Chicago												
Denver												
Evanston												
Fargo												
Acura												
BMW												
Chevrolet												
Dodge												
Edsel												
Fiat												

city	hotel	car

39 THE MODERNS ★★★★

A graduate class in the modern novel focused on ten novels by five different authors ("Lord Jim" and "Nostromo" by Joseph Conrad, "The Bostonians" and "Washington Square" by Henry James, "A Portrait of the Artist as a Young Man" and "Ulysses" by James Joyce, "Sons and Lovers" and "Women in Love" by D.H. Lawrence, and "Mrs. Dalloway" and "To the Lighthouse" by Virginia Woolf). Each novel was taught in conjunction with an assignment (four papers, three in-class essays, two research projects, and one speech). Can you discover the order in which the ten novels were assigned, and the assignment associated with each?

1 No two consecutive novels were by the same author or required the same type of assignment, and no two novels by the same author required the same type of assignment.

2 The second novel was by an author neither of whose novels required an in-class essay.

3 The third novel, which wasn't "Women in Love," required an in-class essay.

4 The fourth novel wasn't "Nostromo."

5 The fifth novel, which wasn't "Washington Square," required a paper.

6 The sixth novel was by either James Joyce or Virginia Woolf.

7 The eighth novel was either "Sons and Lovers" or "To the Lighthouse."

8 The ninth novel, which required a paper, was by an author whose other assigned novel required a speech.

9 The first of the two research projects was on "Ulysses."

10 The third of the four papers that were assigned was on a D.H. Lawrence novel.

11 "Nostromo" was assigned sometime before "Washington Square."

12 "Lord Jim" was assigned sometime after "To the Lighthouse" and sometime before "The Bostonians."

	first	second	third	fourth	fifth	sixth	seventh	eighth	ninth	tenth	four papers	three in-class essays	two research projects	one speech
"Lord Jim" (Conrad)														
"Nostromo" (Conrad)														
"The Bostonians" (James)														
"Washington Square" (James)														
"A Portrait of the Artist ..." (Joyce)														
"Ulysses" (Joyce)														
"Sons and Lovers" (Lawrence)														
"Women in Love" (Lawrence)														
"Mrs. Dalloway" (Woolf)														
"To the Lighthouse" (Woolf)														
four papers														
three in-class essays														
two research projects														
one speech														

order	book	assignment

40 SECRET SANTA ★★★★

Six co-workers (three men, Brad, Jacob, and Max, and three women, Alison, Claudia, and Nancy) held a Secret Santa, in which each person gave a gift to another person, and in turn received a gift from a third person. Can you figure out each person's full name (one is surnamed Hong), the gift each gave, and the person to whom he or she gave it?

1 No pair of people gave each other gifts.

2 Nancy and Whittaker are, in some order, the person who gave the sunglasses and the person who received the picture frame.

3 The three men are: Forbes, the person who received the jewelry box, and the person who received a gift from Claudia.

4 Brad is surnamed Zebatinsky.

5 Jacob either gave or received the keychain.

6 Ms. Schumer either gave or received the video game.

7 Whittaker received a gift from Alison, and gave a gift to the person who gave the jewelry box.

8 Kublicek didn't give a gift to Max.

9 The woman who received the gloves gave a gift to Forbes.

first name	last name	gift given	recipient

Solution, page 91

41 LOST IN TRANSLATION ★★★★

For a model U.N. event, Cora asked eight people to participate in a translation exercise. She placed them in a line, then whispered a message in English to the first person in line. This person translated that message into a different language and whispered it to the second person. Each subsequent person did likewise until the message reached the last translator, who spoke it aloud in English. Discover the order in which the eight people stood in line, the language in which each heard the message, and the language in which each spoke the message.

1 Cora's teacher was either fourth or fifth in line.

2 The person who heard the message in Mandarin spoke it in either Spanish or Vietnamese.

3 Exactly two people stood between, in some order, Cora's friend and cousin.

4 The third person in line spoke the message in French.

5 Cora's friend didn't speak the message in Italian.

6 Her school bus driver spoke the message in Vietnamese.

7 The sixth person in line heard the message in Navajo.

8 Cora's grandmother only speaks two languages: German and Italian.

9 Cora's aunt and her friend are the two people who, in some order, heard and spoke the message in Spanish.

10 Her volleyball coach spoke the message in Mandarin.

11 Her neighbor didn't hear the message in Italian.

place in line	person	language heard	language spoken

Solution, page 92

42 BENCHMARKS ★★★★

The six benches around the central fountain in Wayne Park have each been adopted by one of six different local residents (three men, Charles, Darius, and Ivan, and three women, Anna, Francine, and Sophie), painted a distinctive color, and dedicated to the memory of a different relative. In each case, the proceeds from the adoption were used to restore a different feature of the park (basketball court, game room, tea garden, playground, local history museum, and theater). Can you figure out who adopted each bench, the color it was painted, the relative to whom it was dedicated, and the feature of the park that was improved as a result?

1   The man who funded the renovation of the local history museum didn't adopt bench #2.

2   The purple bench is directly across from the bench that a person dedicated to his or her grandmother, but it isn't adjacent to the bench that Ivan adopted.

3   Bench #3 is painted red.

4   The six people are: Francine, the person who had a bench painted yellow, the person who adopted a bench in memory of his or her father, the person who funded the renovation of the theater, the person who adopted bench #5, and the person who adopted the bench directly across from the one that Ivan adopted.

5   Darius helped to fund the renovation of the tea garden.

6   Bench #6 was dedicated to a beloved uncle.

7   The three women adopted: the blue bench, the bench dedicated to a grandmother, and the bench directly across from the bench whose proceeds funded the game room.

8   The person who funded the playground (who isn't Sophie) didn't paint his or her bench white.

9   The bench dedicated to a beloved aunt wasn't painted blue or yellow.

10 Ivan (who had a bench painted either green or white) funded the improvement of either the basketball court or the playground.

11 Bench #1 wasn't dedicated to an aunt or a grandfather.

12 Anna didn't dedicate a bench to the memory of her mother.

13 The person who funded the game room painted his or her bench either red or purple.

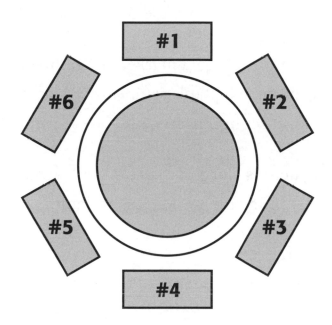

bench	adopter	color	dedicatee	park feature

43 L'AMOUR, L'AMOUR ★★★★

Cheetah Dunbar has acquired renown as a romance novelist. In each of her five novels, a different heroine meets a different attractive stranger in a different outlying locale due to a different disruptive event. See if you can match up each novel with its heroine, hero, setting, and plot point.

1 Either "Eternal Flame" or "Maybe Tomorrow" has a heroine named Paula.

2 Either "Dare to Dream" or "Under the Spell" is set in Rio de Janeiro.

3 The novel whose heroine is Lyddie centers on a plot twist concerning either a crisis in the world's gold market or a military coup.

4 The novel whose heroine is Kat is set in either Marrakech or Tahiti.

5 The plot of the novel set in Singapore revolves around the foiling of a daring bank robbery.

6 The novel whose hero is Hargrove isn't set in Marrakech.

7 "Eternal Flame" is set in either Budapest or Tahiti.

8 Aidan is the hero of the novel centered upon either a military coup or a terrorist plot to derail a train.

9 The novel about Trina is set in either Budapest or Singapore.

10 The five novels are: "Dare to Dream," "Winds of Desire," the novel whose heroine is Kat, the novel whose hero is Scanlon, and the novel whose plot includes a crisis in the world's gold market.

11 The five novels are: "Maybe Tomorrow," the two novels whose heroes are Aidan and Rafael, the novel set in Rio de Janeiro, and the novel whose plot includes a series of assassinations.

12 Either "Maybe Tomorrow" or "Winds of Desire" tells Lyddie's story.

13 Paula (whose love interest isn't Chase) isn't in the novel that's set in Tahiti.

14 Either Rafael or Scanlon falls for Zora.

	Kat	Lyddie	Paula	Trina	Zora	Aidan	Chase	Hargrove	Rafael	Scanlon	Budapest	Marrakech	Rio de Janeiro	Singapore	Tahiti	assassinations	bank robbery	gold market crisis	military coup	train derailment
"Dare to Dream"																				
"Eternal Flame"																				
"Maybe Tomorrow"																				
"Under the Spell"																				
"Winds of Desire"																				
assassinations																				
bank robbery																				
gold market crisis																				
military coup																				
train derailment																				
Budapest																				
Marrakech																				
Rio de Janeiro																				
Singapore																				
Tahiti																				
Aidan																				
Chase																				
Hargrove																				
Rafael																				
Scanlon																				

book	heroine	hero	setting	plot point

44 REUNION RECOLLECTIONS ★★★★

At their tenth high school reunion, six old friends (including Ms. Wolfe) reconnected and caught each other up with their lives. Each person had gone to a different college (including Harvard), then lived in a different country after college before taking up their current job (carpenter, decorative painter, graphic designer, kindergarten teacher, make-up artist, or restaurant manager). Can you link up each woman with her college, the country that she lived in, and her current job?

1 Caroline is surnamed either Briggs or Romo.

2 The woman who lived in Egypt isn't the graphic designer or the restaurant manager.

3 The women who lived in Brazil, India, and Spain are, in some order: Ms. Briggs, the woman who went to the University of Virginia, and the kindergarten teacher.

4 Alison didn't go to San Diego State.

5 Zoe (who isn't Ms. McAllister) is either the decorative painter or the graphic designer.

6 Three of the six women are: Zoe, Ms. Chan, and the woman who went to San Diego State.

7 Four of the six women are: Ms. Torricelli, the woman who went to Duke University, the woman who lived in Japan, and the restaurant manager.

8 Five of the six women are: Bethany, the woman who went to Wellesley, the woman who lived in Japan, the carpenter, and the graphic designer.

9 Kayley didn't live in Brazil.

10 Ms. Torricelli didn't live in India.

11 Caroline didn't go to Egypt or Japan.

12 The kindergarten teacher (who is either Alison or Kayley) went to either Rutgers or San Diego State.

13 The person who lived in Denmark (who isn't Ms. Romo) isn't the make-up artist.

14 Samantha (who lived in either Denmark or Spain) is either the decorative painter or the make-up artist.

Logic Puzzle Grid

	Briggs	Chan	McAllister	Romo	Torricelli	Wolfe	Duke	Harvard	Rutgers	San Diego State	University of Virginia	Wellesley	Brazil	Denmark	Egypt	India	Japan	Spain	carpenter	decorative painter	graphic designer	kindergarten teacher	make-up artist	restaurant manager
Alison																								
Bethany																								
Caroline																									
Kayley																									
Samantha																									
Zoe																									
carpenter																									
decorative painter																									
graphic designer																									
kindergarten teacher																									
make-up artist																									
restaurant manager																									
Brazil																									
Denmark																									
Egypt																									
India																									
Japan																									
Spain																									
Duke																									
Harvard																									
Rutgers																									
San Diego State																									
University of Virginia																									
Wellesley																									

first name	last name	college	country	job

45 CURTAINS FOR YOU ★★★★★

Andrea has recently redecorated all six rooms in her house, finishing all six with matching curtains, in each case in a different material and color (including champagne). Each room has at least one window, and each window in the house is either small or large. Can you figure out the color and material Andrea has chosen for her curtains in each room, and how many small and large windows (if any) each room has?

1   The room with blue curtains has no small windows.

2   The dining room curtains are either cotton or linen.

3   The cotton curtains are either gold or taupe.

4   The guest room has the same number of small and large windows.

5   The room with the silk curtains has only one window, which is small.

6   Five of the six rooms are: the living room, the room with linen curtains, the room with the taupe curtains, a room that has three large windows, and a room that has three small windows

7   The number of large windows in the room with the gold curtains is one less than the number of small windows in that room.

8   Either the bedroom or the library has yellow curtains.

9   The library has fewer than four windows.

10   Andrea's living room has two large windows.

11   The kitchen has either taupe or white curtains.

12   Andrea's bedroom gets the corduroy curtains.

13   All together, the living room and the guest room have a total of five small windows.

14   The room with white curtains has the same number of large windows as one room that has two small windows.

15   The room with the muslin curtains has one large window.

16   The satin curtains are for either Andrea's kitchen or the guest room.

	blue	champagne	gold	taupe	white	yellow	small windows	large windows	corduroy	cotton	linen	muslin	satin	silk
bedroom														
dining room														
guest room														
kitchen														
library														
living room														
corduroy														
cotton														
linen														
muslin														
satin														
silk														
small windows														
large windows														

room	color	fabric	small windows	large windows

46 WINE TASTING ★★★★★

Eight wines were featured at a wine tasting: four whites (Chardonnay, Pinot Grigio, Sauvignon Blanc, and Viognier) and four reds (Cabernet Sauvignon, Malbec, Pinot Noir, and Shiraz). Each had a label of a different color (including lavender). The wines were ranked from 1st to 8th. Can you discover the order in which the wines were tasted, the color of each label, and the ranking that each received?

1   The group tasted all of the white wines before they tasted any of the reds.

2   All participants in the wine tasting received two small sample bottles as a parting gift: the wines with the silver and yellow labels. Of those two wines, the one with the silver label ranked higher.

3   The wine that the group tasted third ranked 6th among those tasted.

4   The Chardonnay was ranked at least two places above the wine that was tasted seventh.

5   One of the wines that the participants received as a parting gift was tasted sometime after the Pinot Grigio and sometime before the wine ranked 1st.

6   The Shiraz ranked immediately below the wine that was tasted first and immediately above the wine with the blue label.

7   The Pinot Noir was tasted immediately before one of the two wines that the participants received as a parting gift.

8   The Viognier ranked either immediately above or immediately below the wine with the orange label.

9   The wine with the gold label wasn't tasted fourth or sixth.

10   Neither the Sauvignon Blanc nor the Cabernet Sauvignon has the tan label.

11   The Viognier was tasted sometime after the wine with the maroon label and sometime before the wine with the blue label.

12   The Malbec ranked 2nd.

13   The Sauvignon Blanc ranked somewhere above the Pinot Grigio.

14   The 5th-ranked wine had either a gold or a tan label.

15   The wine with the silver label wasn't ranked 3rd.

16   The Cabernet Sauvignon ranked somewhere below the wine that was tasted fourth and somewhere above the wine with the maroon label.

		tasted								ranked														
		first	second	third	fourth	fifth	sixth	seventh	eighth	1st	2nd	3rd	4th	5th	6th	7th	8th	blue	gold	lavender	maroon	orange	silver	tan	yellow
white	Chardonnay																								
white	Pinot Grigio																								
white	Sauvignon Blanc																								
white	Viognier																								
red	Cabernet Sauvignon																								
red	Malbec																								
red	Pinot Noir																								
red	Shiraz																								
	blue																								
	gold																								
	lavender																								
	maroon																								
	orange																								
	silver																								
	tan																								
	yellow																								
ranked	1st																								
ranked	2nd																								
ranked	3rd																								
ranked	4th																								
ranked	5th																								
ranked	6th																								
ranked	7th																								
ranked	8th																								

order tasted	wine	label	rank

47 CLOSET CHRONICLES ★★★★★

Following years of putting it off, Molly decided to clean out her closets. On six consecutive days (Monday through Saturday), she enlisted the help of one of her six children (three boys, Ben, Cash, and Jake, and three girls, Katie, Norah, and Tonya) to clean out a different closet. In each case, she found a different item that had been missing for a long time. Can you figure out which day Molly worked with each child, his or her age (each is a different age from 7 to 12), the closet they cleaned out, and the item found there?

1   Tonya is two years older than the child who helped Molly on Monday.

2   On Thursday, Molly and one of her children tackled the office closet.

3   Jake is two years older than the child who helped clean out the laundry room closet.

4   The 12-year-old helped clean the closet in either the dining room or library.

5   Either Ben or Norah is the 8-year-old.

6   The child who helped clean the bedroom closet is two years older than the child who helped clean out the closet where Molly's bridal veil was found.

7   The three girls are: the child Molly worked with on Tuesday, the 11-year-old, and the child who helped clean the hall closet.

8   Molly didn't clean out the library closet on Saturday.

9   Molly's grandmother's recipe book was found on either Monday or Friday.

10 Ben helped his mother at least three days before she cleaned the closet where she found her husband's high school diploma.

11 The child who helped clean the closet where the antique Christmas ornaments were found is at least two years older than the child who helped clean the closet where the photo album was found.

12 The child who helped clean out the dining room closet and the child who helped clean out the closet where Molly's childhood record collection was found are of opposite sexes.

13 Cash helped clean out either the bedroom or office closet.

14 Katie helped out at least two days before the child who helped clean out the laundry room closet.

15 Molly cleaned the hall closet either the day before or the day after she found the family photo album.

	Monday	Tuesday	Wednesday	Thursday	Friday	Saturday	age 7	age 8	age 9	age 10	age 11	age 12	bedroom	dining room	hall	laundry room	library	office	bridal veil	Christmas ornaments	high school diploma	recipe book	record collection	photo album
Ben																								
Cash																								
Jake																								
Katie																								
Norah																								
Tonya																								
bridal veil																								
Christmas ornaments																								
high school diploma																								
recipe book																								
record collection																								
photo album																								
bedroom																			
dining room																			
hall																			
laundry room																			
library																			
office																			
age 7						
age 8						
age 9						
age 10						
age 11						
age 12						

day	child	age	room	item found

Solution, page 94

48 CANDLE-MAKING AT CAMP ★★★★★

At summer camp, six children (three boys named Jordy, Ralph, and Walker, and three girls named Beyoncé, Kylie, and Lauren) learned the art of candle-making. Each child made candles in different shapes, colors, and scents, and each gave his or her candle to a different person. Can you link up each child with the shape, color, and scent of the candle he or she made, and figure out who received each candle?

1 The sky blue candle was shaped like either a pyramid or the Statue of Liberty.

2 The gold candle was scented with either cinnamon or patchouli.

3 Lauren's candle was either maroon or olive green.

4 Walker gave the candle he made to either his rabbi or his sister.

5 The cobalt blue candle was scented with either sandalwood or vanilla.

6 Beyoncé's candle was shaped like either a hand or a pyramid.

7 The three candles that are different shades of blue are: Jordy's candle, the candle shaped like a bunny, and the candle that was given to the piano teacher.

8 The child who made the candle shaped like the Statue of Liberty gave it to either the basketball coach or the rabbi.

9 The uncle didn't receive a candle scented with cinnamon or sandalwood.

10 The candle scented with cinnamon was either gold or olive green.

11 The children who made candles scented with maple and patchouli are of opposite sexes.

12 The child who gave a candle to his or her cousin made either the candle shaped like a bunny or the candle shaped like a car.

13 Ralph gave the candle he made to either his sister or his uncle.

14 The rabbi didn't receive the candle scented with lavender.

15 The navy blue candle was scented with either patchouli or sandalwood.

16 The candle shaped like a car wasn't scented with maple.

17 Kylie's candle was scented with either cinnamon or vanilla.

18 The maroon candle was given to either the basketball coach or the cousin.

19 The children who made the candle shaped like a hand and the vanilla candle are of opposite sexes.

20 The three girls are: the child who made the candle shaped like an owl, the child who made the olive green candle, and the child who gave her candle to her basketball coach.

	bunny	car	hand	owl	pyramid	Statue of Liberty	cobalt blue	gold	maroon	navy blue	olive green	sky blue	cinnamon	lavender	maple	patchouli	sandalwood	vanilla	basketball coach	cousin	piano teacher	rabbi	sister	uncle
Beyoncé																								
Jordy																								
Kylie																								
Lauren																								
Ralph																								
Walker																								
basketball coach																								
cousin																								
piano teacher																								
rabbi																								
sister																								
uncle																								
cinnamon																								
lavender																								
maple																								
patchouli																								
sandalwood																								
vanilla																								
cobalt blue																								
gold																								
maroon																								
navy blue																								
olive green																								
sky blue																								

child	shape	color	scent	recipient

49 EXOTIC PORTS OF CALL ★★★★★

Marion has found that her favorite type of vacation is a sea cruise. In each of the last six years (2009 through 2014), she sailed on a different ship from a different location for a different number of days (from five to ten), in each case during a different month (from January through June). Each time, she made a different friend on the cruise: three women (Clarissa, Shirley, and Yolanda) and three men (Grigori, Hans, and Tobias). For each trip, can you find out the year, month, port of sail, length of the trip, and who she made friends with?

1. Marion's cruise on the Sapphire was the year before her six-day cruise.
2. Her voyage on the Orion occurred later in the year than her voyage out of Curaçao.
3. Her voyage that began in Singapore was longer than the trip where she met Clarissa.
4. Marion's ten-day cruise occurred sometime after her April cruise.
5. The two friends whom Marion met on the Jasmine and on the five-day cruise are of opposite sexes.
6. The voyage out of Marseilles was either two years before or two years after the trip where Marion met Yolanda.
7. Marion's trip on the Albatross was later in the year than the voyage where she met Hans.
8. The 2014 cruise was either two days longer or two days shorter than the cruise that took place in May.
9. The friends whom Marion made on the Empress and on the nine-day cruise are of the same sex.
10. Marion's voyage out of New York occurred sometime after her seven-day cruise.
11. Her trip that began in Istanbul took place earlier in the year than the trip where she met Clarissa.
12. Marion's friend from the Harmony is a man.
13. The 2013 cruise occurred either two months earlier in the year or two months later in the year than the five-day cruise.
14. The trip that started in Bermuda was either three years before or three years after a cruise where Marion met one of the men.
15. Her cruise on the Jasmine was longer than her January cruise.
16. Marion's cruise on the Sapphire lasted three days longer than the cruise that took place in February.
17. She sailed out of Singapore either the year before or the year after she met Grigori.
18. Marion's six cruises were: The 2011 cruise, the cruise on the Orion, the cruise that sailed from Marseilles, the nine-day cruise, the cruise where she met Tobias, and the cruise that occurred in April.
19. Her cruise on the Harmony took place earlier in the year than her ten-day cruise.
20. The cruise that sailed from Curaçao was two days longer than the 2012 cruise and two days shorter than the cruise where Marion met Tobias.

Logic puzzle grid (blank):

	2009	2010	2011	2012	2013	2014	January	February	March	April	May	June	Bermuda	Curaçao	Istanbul	Marseilles	New York	Singapore	five days	six days	seven days	eight days	nine days	ten days	Clarissa	Grigori	Hans	Shirley	Tobias	Yolanda
Albatross																														
Empress																														
Harmony																														
Jasmine																														
Orion																														
Sapphire																														
Clarissa																														
Grigori																														
Hans																														
Shirley																														
Tobias																														
Yolanda																														
five days																														
six days																														
seven days																														
eight days																														
nine days																														
ten days																														
Bermuda																														
Curaçao																														
Istanbul																														
Marseilles																														
New York																														
Singapore																														
January																														
February																														
March																														
April																														
May																														
June																														

year	ship	port	length of trip	friend met	month

Solution, page 95

50 PIZZA PARTY ★★★★★

Eight friends met at a pizza parlor. They sat at a round table, as shown below. Each person ordered a pizza with three toppings, with twelve topping choices available. Each topping was ordered by exactly two people. Can you discover each person's position at the table, his or her full name (one is surnamed Robertson) and occupation, and the three toppings that each ordered?

1 Either Iris or Matthew is surnamed Walters.
2 Nadia and the history teacher are, in some order, the person who sat in seat #2 and the person who sat directly across from Lisa.
3 Scott ordered both ham and onions.
4 Anita and a person who ordered pepperoni are, in some order, the person who sat in seat #4 and the person who sat directly across from the violinist.
5 The person who sat across from Robertson didn't order green peppers.
6 Iris and Lindstrom are, in some order, the person who sat in seat #6 and a person who ordered red peppers.
7 The security guard sat directly between the two people who ordered tomatoes.
8 The merchandiser ordered artichokes.
9 Zanaba sat directly between Nadia and the architect.
10 The eight people are: Eugene, Matthew, Frobisher, Kendall, the architect, the two people who ordered pepperoni, and a person who ordered mushrooms.
11 Either Duchovny or Walters ordered both chicken and tomatoes.
12 Granger and the violinist ordered at least two items in common.
13 One person ordered black olives, green peppers, and sausage.
14 At least one person ordered feta cheese and sausage.
15 The two people who ordered red peppers sat directly across from each other, and one of them is the graphic artist.
16 The eight people are: Brian, Scott, Duchovny, Frobisher, the architect, the bookkeeper, a person who ordered feta cheese, and a person who ordered tomatoes.
17 Matthew sat to the immediate right of Lindstrom.
18 Anita sat next to at least one person who ordered onions.
19 The two people who ordered pepperoni sat next to each other.
20 The four women are: the two people who sat next to the architect, a person who ordered black olives, and a person who ordered chicken.
21 Brian sat directly across from a person who ordered artichokes.
22 The dentist sat directly across from a person who ordered mushrooms.

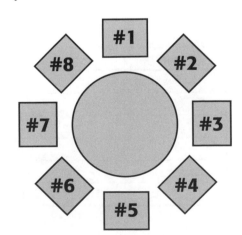

80

Logic puzzle grid with the following column headers (left to right): artichokes, black olives, chicken, feta cheese, green peppers, ham, mushrooms, onions, pepperoni, red peppers, sausage, tomatoes, Duchovny, Frobisher, Granger, Kendall, Lindstrom, Robertson, Walters, Zanaba, architect, bookkeeper, dentist, graphic artist, history teacher, merchandiser, security guard, violinist, seat #1, seat #2, seat #3, seat #4, seat #5, seat #6, seat #7, seat #8

Row labels (top to bottom): Anita, Brian, Eugene, Iris, Lisa, Matthew, Nadia, Scott, seat #1, seat #2, seat #3, seat #4, seat #5, seat #6, seat #7, seat #8, architect, bookkeeper, dentist, graphic artist, history teacher, merchandiser, security guard, violinist, Duchovny, Frobisher, Granger, Kendall, Lindstrom, Robertson, Walters, Zanaba

seat	first name	last name	job	toppings

Solution, page 96

1 SNAIL MAIL

On Wednesday, Kevin received either the credit card offer or the wedding invitation (1). He didn't receive the letter from his grandmother on Thursday or Friday (2). If he had received it on Monday, then he would have received the political mailer on Wednesday (2), which is a contradiction. Therefore, he received the letter from his grandmother on Tuesday and the political mailer on Thursday. He didn't receive the coupon book on Friday (3), so he received it on Monday. He received the credit card offer on Wednesday and the wedding invitation on Friday (1).

Monday	coupon book
Tuesday	letter from grandmother
Wednesday	credit card offer
Thursday	political mailer
Friday	wedding invitation

2 UPSTAIRS, DOWNSTAIRS

The family that lives on the bottom floor isn't surnamed Bryant (1) or Sanchez (2), so they're surnamed Geary. The family that lives on the top floor doesn't have one child (1) or three children (2), so they have two children. Thus, the Geary family has three children (3). By elimination, the family on the middle floor has one child. The Bryant family lives on the top floor (1). By elimination, the Sanchez family lives on the middle floor.

top floor	Bryant	two children
middle floor	Sanchez	one child
bottom floor	Geary	three children

3 BAD MOON RISING

Zinnia dumped her boyfriend because she found out that his rising sign was incompatible with hers (2). She didn't quit her job because Mars entered Aries or because Jupiter went retrograde (3), so it was because Venus sextiled Scorpio. She didn't sell her car because Jupiter went retrograde (1), so this was because Mars entered Aries. By elimination, she changed apartments because Jupiter went retrograde. This wasn't the first week (1) or the third or fourth week (2), so it was the second week. She sold her car the first week (1). She dumped her boyfriend the fourth week (2). By elimination, she quit her job the third week.

week 1	sold her car	Mars entered Aries
week 2	changed apartments	Jupiter went retrograde
week 3	quit her job	Venus sextiled Scorpio
week 4	dumped her boyfriend	incompatible rising signs

4 CHICAGO, WYOMING

The gas station is located at the southwest corner (1). The restaurant is on the southeast corner and Sylvia's business is on the northeast corner (2). Tyler owns the supermarket (3), so this is on the northwest corner. By elimination, the hardware store is on the northeast corner. Kelsey's store isn't on the southwest corner (4), so it's on the southeast corner. By elimination, Lance's store is on the southwest corner.

northwest corner	Tyler	supermarket
northeast corner	Sylvia	hardware store
southwest corner	Lance	gas station
southeast corner	Kelsey	restaurant

5 WORKOUT WARM-UPS

Jacob's fourth warm-up exercise uses the 25-pound weights (1). He doesn't use the 15-pound weights first or second (3), so he uses them third. Thus, he does bench presses second and uses the 10-pound weights first (3). By elimination, he uses the 20-pound weights second. He does curls third and military presses fourth (2). By elimination, he does decline sit-ups first.

first	decline sit-ups	10-pound weights
second	bench presses	20-pound weights
third	curls	15-pound weights
fourth	military presses	25-pound weights

6 CAN YOU HEAR ME NOW?

Alex gets his phone service from EarthNet (2). James doesn't use Telered or WebCon (1), or Hyperion (3), so he uses PhonaFriend. Faith doesn't use Hyperion (3) or Telered (5), so she uses WebCon. Brianna doesn't use Telered (4), so she uses Hyperion. By elimination, Thomas uses Telered, which offers worldwide coverage (4). PhonaFriend, which James uses (see above), doesn't require a contract (1). EarthNet doesn't provide free texting or coverage across multiple devices (2), so it offers rollover minutes. WebCon, which Faith uses (see above) doesn't provide free texting (5), so it provides coverage across multiple devices. By elimination, Hyperion offers free texting.

Alex	EarthNet	rollover minutes
Brianna	Hyperion	free texting
Faith	WebCon	multiple devices
James	PhonaFriend	no contract
Thomas	Telered	worldwide coverage

7 CLASS ACT

Jennifer's fourth class was either chemistry or physics (2). Her sixth class was either U.S. history or world geography (6). English literature and statistics were respectively either second and fifth, or fifth and eighth (1). Thus, Jennifer's fifth class was either English literature or statistics. Thus, she took advanced writing during third period (3). She took pre-calculus during eighth period (5). Her second-period class was English literature and her fifth-period class was statistics (1). Jennifer didn't take physics during first or seventh period (4), so this was her fourth-period class. She didn't take U.S. history during first or seventh period (4), so this was her sixth-period class. World geography was during seventh period (6). By elimination, Jennifer's first-period class was chemistry.

first	chemistry	fifth	statistics
second	English literature	sixth	U.S. history
third	advanced writing	seventh	world geography
fourth	physics	eighth	pre-calculus

8 SPA DAYS

In June, Iris received the Herbal Renewal (1). She didn't receive the Seaweed Wrap in July, August, or September (2), so this was in May. She received a treatment from Magda in August (2). She didn't receive the Body Polish in September (3). If she had received it in July, then she would have received a treatment from Alexis in August (3), which is impossible (see above). Thus, Iris received the Body Polish in August and received a treatment from Alexis in September (3). She received the Javanese Lulur from Talese (4), so this wasn't in May, June, August, or September (see above), so this was in July. By elimination, she received the Ginger Glow from Alexis in September. She received the treatment from Lizzie in May and the treatment from Shania in June (5).

May	Seaweed Wrap	Lizzie
June	Herbal Renewal	Shania
July	Javanese Lulur	Talese
August	Body Polish	Magda
September	Ginger Glow	Alexis

9 WHAT'S THE NEWS?

The five newspapers are: the Herald, the Post, the Fayetteville newspaper, the Maple Creek newspaper, and the paper known predominantly for its real estate section (1). The Tribune is centered in Pottstown (2), so it's known for its real estate section. The Gazette specializes in state politics, and isn't in Maple Creek (4), so it's in Fayetteville. By elimination, the Ledger is in Maple Creek. The Ledger isn't known for its events calendar or its help-wanted section (3), so it's known for local gossip. The Post isn't located in Campbell Lake (6), so the Herald is. By elimination, the Post is located in Williamsburg, and it sells because of its help-wanted section (5). By elimination, the Herald's main attraction is its events calendar.

Campbell Lake Herald	events calendar
Fayetteville Gazette	state politics
Maple Creek Ledger	local gossip
Pottstown Tribune	real estate section
Williamsburg Post	help-wanted section

10 THE GIFT OF TIME

In 2011, Tim received either the sundial or the pendulum clock (5). Either Martina or Wade gave Tim a clock in 2012 (6). He didn't receive the water clock in 2013 or 2014 (2). If he had received it in 2010, then Elizabeth would have given him a clock in 2012 (2), which is a contradiction. Therefore, Tim received the water clock in 2012 and Elizabeth gave him a clock in 2014 (2). Jeremy gave Tim a clock in 2013 and Tim received the sand clock in 2014 (1). Either Geoffrey or Martina gave Tim the spring-powered alarm clock (4), so this was in 2010. He received the sundial in 2011 and the pendulum clock in 2013 (5). Neither Geoffrey nor Wade gave Tim the sundial (3), so Martina did. Thus, Geoffrey gave him the spring-powered alarm clock (4). By elimination, Wade gave him the water clock.

2010	Geoffrey	spring-powered alarm clock
2011	Martina	sundial
2012	Wade	water clock
2013	Jeremy	pendulum clock
2014	Elizabeth	sand clock

11 MOTHER'S DAY ARRANGEMENTS

Three of Natalie's five children are: Sean, Tamara, and the person who sent a chrome flower (5). Eugene sent either the glass or the wood flower (3), and either Ben or Darlene sent silk flowers (7); these two people sent, in some order, roses and tulips (5). Thus, Darlene sent gardenias (1), so she sent a chrome flower, which means Ben sent a silk flower (7). Sean sent a ceramic flower (2). Tamara didn't send a glass flower (6), so Eugene did. Thus, Eugene didn't send roses (4), so he sent tulips. By elimination, Ben sent roses. Also, by elimination, Tamara sent a wooden flower. She didn't send hydrangeas (8), so she sent carnations. By elimination, Sean sent hydrangeas.

Ben	roses	silk
Darlene	gardenias	chrome
Eugene	tulips	glass
Sean	hydrangeas	ceramic
Tamara	carnations	wood

12 NEW TRADITIONALISM

The first and second children who spoke plan to give up Instagram and Skype, in some order (1). Kelly and Patrick spoke, in some order, fourth and fifth (3). Cathy plans to give up Facebook, and she didn't speak third (6), so she spoke sixth. Either Matthew or Teresa plans to give up Amazon Prime (2), so this student spoke third. Lloyd spoke second and the fourth student to speak plans to give up Netflix (5). By elimination, the fifth student to speak plans to give up Twitter. This student isn't Patrick (7), so she's Kelly. Thus, Patrick spoke fourth (3). Teresa didn't speak third (7), so Matthew did. By elimination, Teresa spoke first. She doesn't plan to give up Skype (4), so Lloyd does. By elimination, Teresa plans to give up Instagram.

first	Teresa	Instagram
second	Lloyd	Skype
third	Matthew	Amazon Prime
fourth	Patrick	Netflix
fifth	Kelly	Twitter
sixth	Cathy	Facebook

13 GARDENING PROJECT

The area near the guest house will feature butterfly bushes (1). One part of the yard will have hydrangea bushes and ajugas (2). The area near the swimming pool will bloom each year with poppies (3). The grounds around the treehouse will feature oleanders (4). The area next to the walkway will include black-eyed susans (5). The place to be planted with Carolina allspice will also have daylilies (6). This accounts for the six areas of the garden. The area around the fountain won't include Carolina allspice and daylilies (6), so it will include hydrangea bushes and ajugas. By elimination, the area by the brick wall will include Carolina allspice and daylilies. The area by the swimming pool will not include spireas (3), so it will include potentillas. By elimination, the walkway area will include spireas. The treehouse area will not include crocuses (4), so it will include tulips. By elimination, the guest house area will include crocuses.

brick wall	Carolina allspice	daylilies
fountain	hydrangea bushes	ajugas
guest house	butterfly bushes	crocuses
swimming pool	potentillas	poppies
treehouse	oleanders	tulips
walkway	spireas	black-eyed susans

14 SCIENCE FAIR

The student who won third prize is a girl (1). The fourth-prize topic was either earthquakes or magnetism (6). Ralphie ranked second and the hybridization project ranked fifth (2). Evan ranked fourth and the refraction project ranked third (5). Evan's topic wasn't magnetism (1), so it was earthquakes (6). Ralphie's topic wasn't magnetism or projectiles (1), so it was catalysts. Duncan's project wasn't magnetism or projectiles (1), so it was hybridization. Thus, Duncan's project ranked fifth (see above), so Jennifer's ranked sixth (3). Miriam's project was third (7). By elimination, Bethany's project was first. Her topic wasn't projectiles (4), so it was magnetism. By elimination, Jennifer's topic was projectiles.

first	Bethany	magnetism
second	Ralphie	catalysts
third	Miriam	refraction
fourth	Evan	earthquakes
fifth	Duncan	hybridization
sixth	Jennifer	projectiles

15 SEVEN DEADLY DESSERTS

Jordan baked the second week's cake for either the baby shower or to celebrate her daughter's getting her driver's license (2). The fifth cake she baked was either the Chocolate Envy Cake or the Chocolate Lust Cake (5). She baked the sixth cake for either the baby shower or the birthday party (8). Jordan baked the cake for the bon voyage party the week after she baked the cake for the barbecue and the week before she baked the Chocolate Avarice Cake (6), so she baked the cake for the barbecue the fourth week, the cake for the bon voyage party the fifth week, and the Chocolate Avarice Cake the sixth week. She baked the Chocolate Pride Cake the second week and the cake for the housewarming party the third week (1). She baked the Chocolate Sloth Cake the third week and the cake for the anniversary party the first week (4). She baked the Chocolate Gluttony Cake the seventh week and the cake for the baby shower the sixth week (7). She baked the cake to celebrate her daughter's driver's license the second week (2). By elimination, she baked the cake for the birthday party the seventh week. She baked the Chocolate Lust Cake the first week and the Chocolate Wrath Cake the fourth week (3). By elimination, she baked the Chocolate Envy Cake the fifth week.

first	Chocolate Lust Cake	anniversary
second	Chocolate Pride Cake	driver's license
third	Chocolate Sloth Cake	housewarming
fourth	Chocolate Wrath Cake	barbecue
fifth	Chocolate Envy Cake	bon voyage
sixth	Chocolate Avarice Cake	baby shower
seventh	Chocolate Gluttony Cake	birthday

16 CHORE SCHEDULE

On Monday, one roommate either mops the kitchen floor or vacuums the carpet (2). George does his chore on Friday (7). One roommate takes out the trash on Tuesday, another roommate does the dusting on Wednesday, and Margot does her chore on Thursday (4). Sophie either cleans the bathroom or scrubs the kitchen counters (1), so this is on Sundays. Either Aaron or Edie vacuums the carpet (6), so this is on Mondays. Bridget does the dusting on Wednesday and Margot cleans the bathroom on Thursday (5). Sophie scrubs the kitchen counters on Sunday (1). By elimination, George mops the kitchen floor on Friday. Aaron doesn't do his chore on Tuesday (3), so Edie does. By elimination, Aaron does his chore on Monday.

Sunday	Sophie	scrubbing the kitchen counters
Monday	Aaron	vacuuming the carpet
Tuesday	Edie	taking out the trash
Wednesday	Bridget	dusting
Thursday	Margot	cleaning the bathroom
Friday	George	mopping the kitchen floor

17 RETURN OF THE ALLIGATORS

The first Beatles song that the band performed was either "Lady Madonna" or "Taxman" (1). The second song was "She Loves You," the third was the bass player's song, and the fourth was Marty's song (2). Either the guitarist or pianist sang "Yesterday" (3), so this was fourth. The drummer sang "Taxman" (6), so this was the first song. By elimination, "Lady Madonna" was third. Drew sang this song (4). Thus, Randall didn't play bass, so he played piano (5) and sang second. By elimination, Eddie sang first and Marty played guitar.

first song	"Taxman"	Eddie	drums
second song	"She Loves You"	Randall	piano
third song	"Lady Madonna"	Drew	bass
fourth song	"Yesterday"	Marty	guitar

18 COEN HEADS

The early show on Tuesday was either "Fargo" or "Miller's Crossing" (3). The late show on Monday was either "A Serious Man" or "Inside Llewyn Davis" (7). "O Brother, Where Art Thou?" wasn't the early show on Sunday or Monday (5). If it had been the early show on Wednesday, then "The Hudsucker Proxy" would have been the late show on Monday (5), which is a contradiction. Therefore, "O Brother, Where Art Thou?" was the early show on Thursday and "The Hudsucker Proxy" was the late show on Tuesday. "No Country for Old Men" and "Raising Arizona" were shown on the same day, in some order (1), but not on Wednesday (4), so they were shown on Sunday, with "No Country for Old Men" first (9). "The Big Lebowski" was an early show, but not on Monday (6), so it was shown on Wednesday. "Blood Simple" was the late show on Wednesday (4). "Inside Llewyn Davis" was the early show on Monday (8). "A Serious Man" was the late show on Monday (7). "Fargo" was an early show (2), so this was on Tuesday. By elimination, "Miller's Crossing" was the late show on Thursday.

	early show	late show
Sun.	"No Country for Old Men"	"Raising Arizona"
Mon.	"Inside Llewyn Davis"	"A Serious Man"
Tue.	"Fargo"	"The Hudsucker Proxy"
Wed.	"The Big Lebowski"	"Blood Simple"
Thu.	"O Brother, Where Art Thou?"	"Miller's Crossing"

19 RUN FOR YOUR LIFE

Elaine ran either six or eight miles (6), and so did Blake (3). Patrice ran ten miles and the person who ran to the lighthouse ran four miles (1). Roger ran four miles and the fishing pier is three miles from the starting point (2). Blake ran six miles and Sara ran three (3). Elaine ran eight miles (6). By elimination, Donald ran five miles, and he ran to the yacht club (5). Blake didn't run to the public pool (3) or the café (4), so he ran to the miniature golf course. Elaine, who ran eight miles (see above), ran to the café (4). By elimination, Patrice ran to the public pool.

three miles	Sara	fishing pier
four miles	Roger	lighthouse
five miles	Donald	yacht club
six miles	Blake	miniature golf course
eight miles	Elaine	café
ten miles	Patrice	public pool

20 ERROL'S ERRANDS

Errol's sixth errand was either buying a gift card or mailing a package (9). His second errand was his only stop on Mulberry Street (8). He dropped off the dry cleaning and picked up a prescription consecutively, though not necessarily in that order, on the same street (1), so he did these errands either third and fourth or fourth and fifth. In either case, his fourth errand was either dropping off the dry cleaning or picking up a prescription. He paid the electric bill second and returned the toaster fifth (2). Thus, his third errand was either dropping off the dry cleaning or picking up a prescription (see above). He bought fruit seventh and ran an errand on Union Avenue sixth (7). Errol mailed a package on either Third Avenue or Wendell Way (3), so this was his first errand. By elimination, he bought the gift card sixth. His seventh errand was on Hyacinth Boulevard (4). His third errand wasn't on Grandview Terrace or Third Avenue (6), so it was on Wendell Way. His fourth errand was also on Wendell Way (see above). His first errand was on Third Avenue (3). By elimination, his fifth errand was on Grandview Terrace. He didn't drop off the dry cleaning fourth (5), so he did this third. By elimination, he picked up the prescription fourth.

first errand	package	Third Avenue
second errand	electric bill	Mulberry Street
third errand	dry cleaning	Wendell Way
fourth errand	prescription	Wendell Way
fifth errand	toaster	Grandview Terrace
sixth errand	gift card	Union Avenue
seventh errand	fruit	Hyacinth Boulevard

21 TAROT INSPIRATION

On Tuesday and Wednesday, Drake chose the Queen of Pentacles and the Prince of Swords, not necessarily in that order (4). He chose the King of Swords and Queen of Wands on consecutive days, but not Sunday and Monday (7). Thus, he chose these two cards on either Thursday and Friday, or Friday and Saturday. In either case, he chose either the King of Swords or the Queen of Wands on Friday. He chose the Prince of Wands on Sunday, the Princess of Cups on Monday, and the Wheel on Tuesday (1). He chose the Hierophant on Thursday and the Princess of Pentacles on Saturday (6). He chose the Chariot on Wednesday, the King of Swords on Thursday, and the Queen of Wands on Friday (7). He also chose the Tower on Friday (3). He chose the Star on Sunday and the Fool on Monday (5). By elimination, he chose the Moon on Saturday. He didn't choose the Prince of Swords on Wednesday (2), so this was on Tuesday. By elimination, he chose the Queen of Pentacles on Wednesday.

Sunday	The Star	Prince of Wands
Monday	The Fool	Princess of Cups
Tuesday	The Wheel	Prince of Swords
Wednesday	The Chariot	Queen of Pentacles
Thursday	The Hierophant	King of Swords
Friday	The Tower	Queen of Wands
Saturday	The Moon	Princess of Pentacles

22 MEETING UP

On Monday, Sandra went to the meet-up for Portuguese speakers (1). On Friday, she attended the meet-up at Bean and Nothingness (8). She went to the meet-up for cat lovers on Tuesday, met Raoul on Wednesday, and went to Café Caffeine on Thursday (4). The meet-up for amateur photographers was at Jumpin' Java (7), so this was on Wednesday. The meet-up at Joe to Go was on Tuesday and the one for bridge players was on Thursday (2). By elimination, Sandra went to the meet-up for knitting enthusiasts on Friday, and this is where Sandra met either Joyce or Tony (3). Also by elimination, she went to the meet-up at the King of Cups on Monday. She didn't meet Cassius at Joe to Go or the King of Cups (6), so she met him on Thursday at Café Caffeine. She met Joyce on Tuesday and Leo on Monday (5). By elimination, she met Tony on Friday.

Mon.	King of Cups	Leo	Portuguese speakers
Tue.	Joe to Go	Joyce	cat owners
Wed.	Jumpin' Java	Raoul	amateur photogs
Thu.	Café Caffeine	Cassius	bridge players
Fri.	Bean & Nothingness	Tony	knitting enthusiasts

23 BINGE-WATCHING

In February and July, Seymour watched "House of Cards" and "Mad Men," in some order (4). During three consecutive months, he watched "Californication," "Homeland," and "True Blood," in some order (8), which must have been either March through May or April through June. Thus, he watched one of these shows in April and another in May. Lillian didn't watch any of the three shows Seymour could have watched in May (8), so he didn't watch "Game of Thrones" in June (2), so he watched "Game of Thrones" in March, a show with Lillian in February, and a show with Trevor in May (2). In June, he watched "Californication," "Homeland," or "True Blood" (8). He watched "Breaking Bad" in August and a show with Patrick in July (1). By elimination, he watched "Dexter" in January, but not with Keith or Wanda (6), and not with Jeremy or Rhonda, who watched shows in March and April in some order (5), so he watched it with Augie. He watched "Homeland" with Keith (3), so this was in June. By elimination, he watched "Breaking Bad" in August with Wanda. He didn't watch "Mad Men" in July (9), so he watched "House of Cards" in July and watched "Mad Men" in February (4). He didn't watch "Game of Thrones" in March with Rhonda (9), so he watched that with Jeremy, and watched a show with Rhonda in April. This show wasn't "True Blood" (7), so it was "Californication." By elimination, Seymour watched "True Blood" in May.

January	Augie	"Dexter"
February	Lillian	"Mad Men "
March	Jeremy	"Game of Thrones"
April	Rhonda	"Californication"
May	Trevor	"True Blood"
June	Keith	"Homeland"
July	Patrick	"House of Cards"
August	Wanda	"Breaking Bad"

24 BETTER LATTE THAN NEVER

Hope and the person surnamed Banks received the items that each other ordered (5). Eugene received the item that DuBois ordered, and Thompson received the item that Eugene ordered (8). This accounts for five of the six people. Arnold is surnamed either Reeves or Valentino (3), so he's the sixth person. If DuBois had received the item that Thompson ordered, then Arnold would have received his own order, which is impossible (1). Thus, DuBois received what Arnold ordered, and Arnold received what Thompson ordered. Jimmy ordered the decaf latte, but a woman received it (2), so Jimmy isn't DuBois or Thompson, so he's Banks. Thus, Hope received the decaf latte (5). Schumacher received either the café Borgia or the double espresso (9), so he's Eugene. Thus, DuBois ordered either the café Borgia or the double espresso. Felicia ordered either the French-pressed coffee or the macchiato (4), so she's Thompson. Thus, Arnold received either the French-pressed coffee or the macchiato. By elimination, Pandora is DuBois. She received the depth charge (10), so Arnold ordered it. Reeves ordered either the café Borgia or the French-pressed coffee (7), so she's Hope. Therefore, Jimmy Banks received either the café Borgia or the French-pressed coffee (5). By elimination, Arnold is Valentino. He didn't receive the macchiato (6), so he received the French-pressed coffee and Felicia ordered it (see above). Thus, Hope Reeves ordered the café Borgia and Jimmy Banks received it (see above). So Pandora DuBois ordered the double espresso and Eugene Schumacher received it (see above). By elimination, Eugene Schumacher ordered the macchiato and Felicia Thompson received it.

	ordered	received
Arnold Valentino	depth charge	French press
Eugene Schumacher	macchiato	double espresso
Felicia Thompson	French press	macchiato
Hope Reeves	café Borgia	decaf latte
Jimmy Banks	decaf latte	café Borgia
Pandora DuBois	double espresso	depth charge

25 COSTUME PARTY

Either Bryan or Victor arrived third (3). The last two children to arrive at the party were both boys (9). Three children who arrived in consecutive order were Eric, the child who dressed as a ghost, and the child who dressed as a princess (5). A girl dressed as the princess (1), so these three arrived either second, third, and fourth or fourth, fifth, and sixth. Thus, the fourth child to arrive was either Eric or the girl who dressed as the princess. In either case, the girl who dressed as a witch (1) didn't arrive fourth, so she arrived first (7). The boy dressed as Batman (1) and Angela arrived in consecutive order (6), so they arrived third and fourth, fourth and fifth, or fifth and sixth. But since three boys arrived third, seventh, and eighth, and Eric arrived either second or fourth, girls must have arrived fifth and sixth. This means the boy dressed as Batman cannot have arrived fifth, so he arrived third or fourth. If Eric, then, had arrived second, the children dressed as the ghost and princess would have arrived third and fourth (5), which is a contradiction. Therefore, Eric arrived fourth, the child who dressed as a ghost arrived fifth, and the girl who dressed as a princess arrived sixth. Angela arrived fifth and the boy who wore the Batman costume arrived fourth (6). By elimination, a girl arrived second. A boy dressed as Spider-Man (1), so he arrived seventh and the boy who arrived eighth wore a robot costume (10). This boy isn't Jack (2), so Jack arrived seventh. Victor didn't arrive eighth (11), so Bryan did. By elimination, Victor arrived third. He didn't dress as a vampire (11), so the child who wore the vampire costume arrived second. By elimination, Victor dressed as a clown. Since he arrived third, Iris arrived second (4). Maria arrived first and Wendy arrived sixth (8).

first	Maria	witch
second	Iris	vampire
third	Victor	clown
fourth	Eric	Batman
fifth	Angela	ghost
sixth	Wendy	princess
seventh	Jack	Spider-Man
eighth	Bryan	robot

26 PEANUT BETTER SANDWICHES

Josh made the sandwich with pickles exactly three days before he made the sandwich with whitefish (2), so he made the sandwich with whitefish on either Thursday or Friday. He made the sandwich with olives exactly three days before he made the sandwich with anchovies (7), so he also made the sandwich with anchovies on either Thursday or Friday. But he didn't mix anchovies with whitefish (4), so he ate one of these two items on Thursday and the other on Friday. Therefore, he ate pickles (2) and olives (7) on Monday and Tuesday, in some order. One sandwich included bacon and peaches (1), so this was on Wednesday. His sandwich on Tuesday included sardines and his sandwich on Thursday included tartar sauce (5). Tuesday's sandwich also included either pickles or olives (see above), so Friday's sandwich included pesto (6). His sandwiches on Monday and Tuesday included pickles and olives, in some order (see above), and his sandwiches on Thursday and Friday included whitefish and anchovies, in some order (see above). Thus, by elimination, Monday's sandwich included raisins, so it didn't include olives (3); therefore, Tuesday's sandwich included olives and Friday's included anchovies (7). His sandwich on Monday included pickles and his sandwich on Thursday included whitefish.

Monday	raisins and pickles
Tuesday	sardines and olives
Wednesday	bacon and peaches
Thursday	tartar sauce and whitefish
Friday	pesto and anchovies

27 PETTING ZOO

The three animals housed in pens #2, #4, and #7 are, in some order, ducks, rabbits, and sheep (3). Kate, William, and Zach chose, in some order, the animals housed in pens #2, #5, and #8 as their favorite animals (7). The chickens are housed in pen #3 and Simon's favorite type of animal is kept in pen #7 (6). Juan's favorite type of animal is in pen #6 (1). Martin's favorite type of animal is in #3 and the rabbits are in pen #7 (8). Emily's favorite type of animal is

in pen #4 (4). William's favorite type of animal lives in pen #5 and Alison's in pen #1 (9). Pigs are Zach's favorite type of animal (2), and are housed in pen #8 (7). By elimination, Kate's favorite type of animal is in pen #2. The llamas are housed in pen #1 (10). The sheep are housed in pen #2 and the donkeys in pen #6 (5). The ducks are housed in pen #4 (3). By elimination, the goats are housed in pen #5.

pen #1	pen #2	pen #3	pen #4
Alison	Kate	Martin	Emily
llamas	sheep	chickens	ducks

pen #5	pen #6	pen #7	pen #8
William	Juan	Simon	Zach
goats	donkeys	rabbits	pigs

28 DOG DAYS

On Tuesday, Abby visited either Jordan or Miguel (7). She visited Susan on Monday and the person with the dachshund on Thursday (4). She visited Wayne on Wednesday, the person who owns Spunky on Thursday, and the person who owns the sheepdog on Friday (1). Vicki owns Baby (6), so Abby visited her on Friday. She visited Miguel on Tuesday and the person who owns the cocker spaniel on Wednesday (2). By elimination, she visited Jordan on Thursday. Wayne owns Pepper (3). Susan owns the Yorkshire terrier and Miguel owns Falafel (5). By elimination, Susan owns Cha-Cha and Miguel owns the beagle.

Monday	Susan	Cha-Cha	Yorkshire terrier
Tuesday	Miguel	Falafel	beagle
Wednesday	Wayne	Pepper	cocker spaniel
Thursday	Jordan	Spunky	dachshund
Friday	Vicki	Baby	sheepdog

29 KEYS TO REBECCA

The seven keys are: the keys to the garage, the in-laws' apartment, and the storage room; the blue, red, and white keys; and the sixth key on the ring (5). The silver key opens either the attic or the basement (6), so this is the sixth key on the ring. The storage room key is fifth and the red key is fourth (4). The garage key is third (7). The second key on the ring is either gold or purple (2), so this is the key to the in-laws' apartment. By elimination, the blue and white keys are, in some order, the first and seventh keys. The blue key isn't the first key (3), so it's the seventh key and the attic key is sixth (3). Thus, the white key is first (see above). The yellow key is third and the gold key is second (8). By elimination, the purple key is fifth. The office key is fourth (8). The first key doesn't open the front door (1), so it opens the basement. By elimination, the seventh key opens the front door.

first	basement	white
second	in-laws' apartment	gold
third	garage	yellow
fourth	office	red
fifth	storage room	purple
sixth	attic	silver
seventh	front door	blue

30 ROLL PLAY

The child who wrapped dimes is 10 years old (3). The child who wrapped 11 rolls of coins is an odd number of years old (4). One child wrapped an even number of rolls of quarters (6). Todd, who is 8 years old, wrapped either pennies or nickels (7). This accounts for the four children. Lydia wrapped 9 rolls of coins (1), so she's 10 years old. She's two years younger than one of the other children (1), so one of the children is 12 years old. Therefore, this child wrapped quarters, so another child is 11 years old (6). That child must be the one who wrapped 11 rolls of coins (see above). He isn't Stephen (2), so Stephen is 12 years old. By elimination, Melanie is 11 years old. One of the other children wrapped 12 rolls of coins (8), but not Stephen (2), so that was Todd. Thus, there were 12 rolls of pennies and 11 rolls of nickels (9). There were either 7 or 8 rolls of some type of coin (5), which by elimination was quarters. There were an even number of quarters (6), so there were 8 rolls of quarters.

Lydia	10 years old	9 rolls of dimes
Melanie	11 years old	11 rolls of nickels
Stephen	12 years old	8 rolls of quarters
Todd	8 years old	12 rolls of pennies

31 SLAMMING POETRY

The first poet to read punctuated his or her poem with a sequence of loud, piercing screams (1). Arlo read third (6). "Kittens and Puppies" was the sixth poem to be read (8). Mary Jo didn't read first or sixth (3). If she had read second, then the person who hopped on one foot would have read first (3), which is a contradiction. And if Mary Jo had read fifth, then "Blissful Remembrance" would have been sixth (3), which is a contradiction. Thus, Mary Jo read fourth, so "Blissful Remembrance" was fifth (3). Tamarynd read "Grace Under Pressure" while banging her head with a rubber mallet (2), so this was second. Arlo read while hopping on one foot (3). The author of "Fingers on the Blackboard" read while cracking eggs over his or her head (7), so this was Mary Jo. Victor read sixth and the person who read while blindfolded was fifth (4). By elimination, Victor read while beating his chest. Claire didn't read "Blissful Remembrance" (5), so Blake did. By elimination, Claire read first. She didn't read "Naturally, I'm Chagrined" (5), so Arlo did. By elimination, Claire read "Lost and Not Found."

first	Claire	"Lost and Not Found"	screaming
second	Tamarynd	"Grace Under Pressure"	mallet
third	Arlo	"Naturally, I'm Chagrined"	hopping
fourth	Mary Jo	"Fingers on the Blackboard"	eggs
fifth	Blake	"Blissful Remembrance"	blindfold
sixth	Victor	"Kittens and Puppies"	chest

32 LIT UP

Georgia's eight stories are: "A Cross to Bear," "Have You Got an Umbrella?," and "Vigilant Love"; the stories published in Athena Magazine, Rhode Island Review, and Word Up; and the stories published in October 2013 and March 2014 (9). "Better Cheer Up" wasn't published in Word Up or Athena Magazine (3), and it was published between November 2013 to February 2014 inclusive (3), so it was published in Rhode Island Review. "My Side" was published in either November 2013 or January 2014 (1), so it was published in either Athena Magazine or Word Up. If "Better Cheer Up" had been published in December 2013, then the story in Word Up would have been published in October 2013 (3), which is impossible (9). If "Better Cheer Up" had been published in January 2014, then the story in Athena Magazine would have been published in March 2014 (3), which is impossible (9). Thus, "Better Cheer Up" was published in either November 2013 or February 2014, the story in Word Up was published in either September 2013 or December 2013, and the story in Athena Magazine was published in either January 2014 or April 2014 (3). Since "My Side" was published in either Word Up or Athena Magazine (see above), it must have been published in Athena Magazine in January 2014 (1).

"Better Cheer Up" was published in November 2013 and the story in Word Up was published in September 2013 (3). By elimination, "A Cross to Bear," "Have You Got an Umbrella?," and "Vigilant Love" were published, in some order, in December 2013, February 2014, and April 2014 (9). "Three-Legged Stool Pigeon" was published in March 2014 and the story in South Carolina Quarterly appeared in February 2014 (5). "If You Want to Know the Truth …" was published in either 27 Letters or Neverending Stories (2), so this was in October 2013. By elimination, "Left to Your Own Devices" was published in September 2013. The story in Neverending Stories was published in 2014 (8), so this was in March 2014 and "Vigilant Love" was published in April 2014 (4). "If You Want to Know the Truth …" was published in 27 Letters (2). Golden Gate Gazette didn't publish Georgia's story in December of 2013 (6), so it published "Vigilant Love" in April 2014. By elimination, Post-Punk Playbook published her story in December 2013. "Have You Got an Umbrella?" wasn't published in Post-Punk Playbook (7), so it was published in South Carolina Quarterly. By elimination, "A Cross to Bear" was published in Post-Punk Playbook.

Sep. '13	"Left to Your Own Devices"	Word Up
Oct. '13	"If You Want to Know the Truth …"	27 Letters
Nov. '13	"Better Cheer Up"	Rhode Island Review
Dec. '13	"A Cross to Bear"	Post-Punk Playbook
Jan. '14	"My Side"	Athena Magazine
Feb. '14	"Have You Got an Umbrella?"	South Carolina Quarterly
Mar. '14	"Three-Legged Stool Pigeon"	Neverending Stories
Apr. '14	"Vigilant Love"	Golden Gate Gazette

33 CHILI TODAY

The six winners were: Andrew, Dakins, the person whose chili includes lima beans, the fourth-place winner, the person whose chili ranked just ahead of Sarah, and the person whose chili ranked just behind McNeill (10). The sixth-place winner wasn't Dakins (2), Andrew (5), or the person who used lima beans (7), so the sixth-place winner ranked just behind McNeill (10). Thus, McNeill ranked fifth, so the chili with grapefruit juice ranked fourth (1). Sarah's secret ingredient is either blueberry preserves or vermouth, and she isn't Dakins (2). So, of the six winners mentioned in clue 10, Sarah is the person whose chili ranked just behind McNeill; therefore, Sarah's chili ranked sixth (see above). So, of the six winners mentioned in clue 10, the person whose chili ranked just ahead of Sarah's was McNeill, the fifth-place winner. Either Phelps or Watkins includes white chocolate as a secret ingredient (6), so this is Andrew. By elimination, the chili with lima beans ranked among the top three, so the chili with sauerkraut didn't rank fifth (7), so Dakins made this chili. Thus, this chili also ranked among the top three (see above). So, either the chili with sauerkraut or the chili with lima beans ranked second (7). Thus, Scholler ranked second (3), so Andrew's chili ranked first (5). The chili with lima beans ranked second and the chili with sauerkraut ranked third (7). The chili with white chocolate ranked two places ahead of Kathleen's chili (3), so Kathleen's chili is the third-ranking chili with sauerkraut. Geoffrey's chili includes vermouth (9), so it ranked fifth. By elimination, the sixth-ranked chili includes blueberry preserves. Watkins's chili includes neither blueberry preserves nor grapefruit juice (4), so it includes white chocolate. Scholler isn't Nick (8), so Lorraine is Scholler, so her chili was ranked second (see above). By elimination, Nick's chili was ranked fourth. Nick isn't Zenakis (8), so he's Phelps. By elimination, Sarah is Zenakis.

1st	Andrew Watkins	white chocolate
2nd	Lorraine Scholler	lima beans
3rd	Kathleen Dakins	sauerkraut
4th	Nick Phelps	grapefruit juice
5th	Geoffrey McNeill	vermouth
6th	Sarah Zenakis	blueberry preserves

34 DAILY BREAD

The six bread orders were, in some order: the orders for ciabatta and Granary bread, the orders for 20 and 30 loaves, and the fifth and sixth orders (4). The order for Irish soda bread wasn't fifth or sixth (1) and was for more than 20 loaves (9), so it was for 30 loaves. The fifth order contained fewer than 30 loaves, but not 15 (9), so it contained 25 loaves. The order for Jewish rye was for 35 loaves (2), so this was sixth, and the second order was for 20 loaves. They filled the order for the wedding fifth (8). The pumpernickel order was for either the conference or the farewell party (5), so this was the order for 20 loaves. By elimination, the order for the French baguettes was fifth. They filled the order for the camping trip sixth (6). The order for the picnic was for 15 loaves (9), so it wasn't for ciabatta (7), so it was for Granary bread, and was either third or fourth. By elimination, the order for ciabatta was for 40 loaves. This wasn't for the conference, and neither was the order for Irish soda bread (1), so the pumpernickel was for the conference. This was the second order, so the order for Irish soda bread was filled first (1). The order for the graduation was for 40 loaves and the order for the farewell party was for 30 (10). The order for the graduation was filled third and the order for Granary bread was filled fourth (3).

first	farewell party	Irish soda bread	30 loaves
second	conference	pumpernickel	20 loaves
third	graduation	ciabatta	40 loaves
fourth	picnic	Granary bread	15 loaves
fifth	wedding	French baguettes	25 loaves
sixth	camping trip	Jewish rye	35 loaves

35 LOOKING FOR DIRECTION

Emma's fifth turn was a left turn (4). Her turn onto Bates Road wasn't at the amusement park and wasn't her fifth turn (9), so it wasn't any of her three left turns (4); therefore, it was a right turn. Thus, her second turn was a left turn (1). It wasn't at the amusement park (9), so it was onto Hollywood Avenue (4). So far, we have accounted for two of the three left turns. The remaining left turn was at the amusement park (4), but this wasn't Emma's first turn (9), so her first turn was to the right. This was onto Sullivan Street (2). Thus, to recap, two of the three right turns were her first turn onto Sullivan Street and her turn onto Bates Road, and the three left turns were the second turn onto Hollywood Avenue, the fifth turn, and the turn at the amusement park. Thus, we have enumerated five of Emma's six turns. Her turn at the ice cream stand was onto either Piedmont Pike or Villanova Way, and was either third or sixth (7), so this is the remaining turn in our enumeration; therefore, it's a right turn. Her turn onto Kendall Drive was at either a car wash or a pharmacy (3), so this was Emma's fifth turn. Her fourth turn was at the museum (8), so this was onto Bates Road. Her sixth turn was at the amusement park (9), and this was a left turn (see above). By elimination, her third turn was a right turn at the ice cream stand. Thus, she made a left turn at the furniture store (6), so this was her second turn. Her third turn wasn't onto Piedmont Pike (5), so it was onto Villanova Way. By elimination, her sixth turn was onto Piedmont Pike. Her fifth turn wasn't at the car wash (5), so it was at the pharmacy. By elimination, her first turn was at the car wash.

first	Sullivan Street	right	car wash
second	Hollywood Avenue	left	furniture store
third	Villanova Way	right	ice cream stand
fourth	Bates Road	right	museum
fifth	Kendall Drive	left	pharmacy
sixth	Piedmont Pike	left	amusement park

36 COLORFUL KARAOKE

The six people are: Douglas, the person surnamed Tan, the person who sang "Bad, Bad Leroy Brown," the person who sang "Heart of Gold," the person who wore gray, and the person who wore white (6). The person surnamed Gray sang "White Rabbit" (4), so he or she didn't wear gray or white (1), so this person is Douglas. The person who sang "Atom Tan" isn't surnamed Tan (1) and didn't wear gray (2), so he or she wore white. The person who sang "All Cats Are Gray" didn't wear gray (1), so he or she is surnamed Tan. By elimination, the person who wore gray sang "Black Velvet." The person surnamed Brown didn't sing "Bad, Bad Leroy Brown" (1), didn't sing "Atom Tan" (2), and didn't wear gray (2), so he or she sang "Heart of Gold." The person surnamed White didn't wear white (1) or gray (2), so he or she sang "Bad, Bad Leroy Brown." So far, we have enumerated four of the six people mentioned in clue 2. Thus, Elaine is surnamed Tan, and Douglas Gray wore black (2). Since the person surnamed Brown sang "Heart of Gold" (see above), he or she didn't wear brown or gold (1), so he or she wore tan. The person who sang "Bad, Bad Leroy Brown" didn't wear brown (1), so he or she wore gold. By elimination, Elaine Tan wore brown. The person surnamed Black didn't sing "Black Velvet" (1), so he or she sang "Atom Tan." By elimination, the person surnamed Gold sang "Black Velvet." Her first name is Beverly and Arnold's last name is Black (3). If Chuck were surnamed Brown, then by elimination Frances would be surnamed White, so she would have sung "Bad, Bad Leroy Brown" (see above). But this is impossible (5), so Chuck is surnamed White. By elimination, Frances is surnamed Brown.

Arnold Black   "Atom Tan"   white clothes
Beverly Gold   "Black Velvet"   gray clothes
Chuck White   "Bad, Bad Leroy Brown"   gold clothes
Douglas Gray   "White Rabbit"   black clothes
Elaine Tan   "All Cats Are Gray"   brown clothes
Frances Brown   "Heart of Gold"   tan clothes

37 PUBLIC SPEAKING

The 7-minute speech was about the mating habits of penguins (3). Tomas gave the 8-minute speech (8). The speech about a family wedding was 8 minutes, the second speech was 9 minutes, and Sharon's speech was 10 minutes (4). The 6-minute speech was first (2). Rodney's speech was either third or fourth (2), so it was the 7-minute speech. The speech about hang gliding was 6 minutes (6), so it was first (see above). The speech about angels was second, the vocal variety speech was third, Tomas's speech was fourth, and the 10-minute speech was fifth (7)—and, by elimination, the 10-minute speech was about starting a business. Rodney's speech was third (see above). The eye-contact speech was second (2). Ursula was working on body language (1), so her speech was first. By elimination, Victoria's speech was second. Sharon was working on her slideshow presentation (5). By elimination, Tomas was working on organization of main points.

first	Ursula	hang gliding	body language	6 min.
second	Victoria	angels	eye contact	9 min.
third	Rodney	penguins	vocal variety	7 min,
fourth	Tomas	wedding	organization	8 min.
fifth	Sharon	business	slide show	10 min.

38 ABCS OF BUSINESS TRAVEL

Natalie rented the Edsel in either Chicago or Fargo, and stayed during that trip at either the Aston International or the Fairfield Inn (2). When Natalie stayed at the Crowne Plaza, which was in either Denver or Evanston, she rented either the Acura or the Dodge (7). In Austin, where Natalie stayed either at the Days Inn or the Embassy Suites, she rented either a Chevrolet or a Fiat (9). This accounts for three of the six business trips. The remaining three trips were to Baltimore, the place where Natalie stayed at the Best Western, and the place where she rented the BMW (1). In Fargo, Natalie didn't stay at the Best Western (5), and didn't rent a BMW (8), so this was the trip where she rented the Edsel (see above). She didn't stay at the Fairfield Inn there (1), so she stayed at the Aston International. When she stayed at the Fairfield Inn, she didn't rent a BMW (6), so she was in Baltimore. She didn't rent a Fiat on this trip (1), or when she stayed at the Best Western (3), so she rented the Fiat in Austin. On this trip, she didn't stay at the Days Inn (3), so she stayed at the Embassy Suites. By elimination, she stayed at the Days Inn when she rented the BMW. This wasn't in Denver (1), nor did she stay at the Best Western in Denver (5), so she stayed at the Crowne Plaza in Denver. She didn't rent a Dodge in Denver (1), so she rented an Acura. Thus, she didn't rent a Dodge when she stayed at the Best Western (4), so she rented a Dodge in Baltimore. By elimination, she rented a Chevrolet when she stayed at the Best Western. This wasn't in Chicago (1), so it was in Evanston. By elimination, she stayed at the Days Inn in Chicago.

Austin	Embassy Suites	Fiat
Baltimore	Fairfield Inn	Dodge
Chicago	Days Inn	BMW
Denver	Crowne Plaza	Acura
Evanston	Best Western	Chevrolet
Fargo	Aston International	Edsel

39 THE MODERNS

The third assignment was an in-class essay (3). The fifth assignment was a paper (5), and so was the ninth (8). Neither of the two remaining papers was the fourth, sixth, eighth, or tenth assignment (1), so one of them was the seventh assignment and the other was either the first or the second assignment. Thus, the seventh assignment was the third of the four papers, so it was on a D.H. Lawrence novel (10). Thus, the eighth novel wasn't "Sons and Lovers" (1), so it was "To the Lighthouse" (7). "Lord Jim" was assigned ninth and "The Bostonians" was assigned tenth (12). "Nostromo" required a speech (8), and it wasn't assigned fourth (4) or sixth (6), so it was assigned either first or second. Thus, the first and second assignments were, in some order, a paper and the speech on "Nostromo" (see above), which was the only speech. The fourth assignment wasn't an in-class essay (1), so it was a research project. Thus, it was the first of the two research projects, so it was on "Ulysses" (9). We already know that the seventh assignment was a paper on a D.H. Lawrence novel (see above), so the other D.H. Lawrence novel didn't also require a paper (1). Thus, this novel wasn't assigned first or second ("Nostromo" and a paper, per above) or fifth (another paper) or sixth (1), so it was assigned third. That book wasn't "Women in Love" (3), so it was "Sons and Lovers," and the seventh book was "Women in Love." We know the fourth novel was "Ulysses," so the fifth novel wasn't "A Portrait of the Artist as a Young Man" (1), nor was it "Washington Square" (5), so it was "Mrs. Dalloway." The sixth novel was "A Portrait of the Artist as a Young Man" (6). The speech on "Nostromo" was assigned first and "Washington Square" was the second novel (11), for which a paper was required (see above). "The Bostonians" didn't require an in-class essay (2), so it required a research project. By elimination, "A Portrait of the Artist as a Young Man" and "To the Lighthouse" both required in-class essays.

first	"Nostromo," Joseph Conrad	speech
second	"Washington Square," Henry James	paper
third	"Sons and Lovers," D. H. Lawrence	in-class essay
fourth	"Ulysses," James Joyce	research project
fifth	"Mrs. Dalloway," Virginia Woolf	paper
sixth	"A Portrait of the Artist ...," James Joyce	in-class essay
seventh	"Women in Love," D. H. Lawrence	paper
eighth	"To the Lighthouse," Virginia Woolf	in-class essay
ninth	"Lord Jim," Joseph Conrad	paper
tenth	"The Bostonians," Henry James	research project

40 SECRET SANTA

Alison gave a gift to Whittaker, and Whittaker gave a gift to the person who gave the jewelry box (7). A man received the jewelry box (3). This accounts for four different people. If the man who received the jewelry box had given a gift to Alison, then by elimination, the remaining two people would have given gifts to each other, which is impossible (1). Therefore, the man who received the jewelry box gave a gift to a fifth person, who gave a gift to a sixth person, and this sixth person gave a gift to Alison. Whittaker received a gift from Alison and didn't receive the jewelry box (see above), so Whittaker isn't mentioned in clue 3; therefore, Whittaker is a woman. She isn't Nancy (2), so she's Claudia. The person who gave the jewelry box received a gift from Claudia (see above), so a man gave the jewelry box (3). Forbes is a man, but he didn't give or receive the jewelry box (3). He received a gift from a woman (9), so he didn't receive a gift from the man who received the jewelry box (see above); therefore, Mr. Forbes gave a gift to Alison. He received a gift from a woman (9), so this woman is Nancy; therefore, Nancy received the gloves from the man who received the jewelry box (see above). The gift Nancy gave Mr. Forbes was the sunglasses, and Claudia Whittaker received the picture frame from Alison (2). Ms. Schumer either gave or received the video game (6), so that's not Nancy, which means Alison is Schumer, and she received the video game from Mr. Forbes. By elimination, Claudia Whittaker gave the keychain to the person who gave the jewelry box. Jacob received the keychain (5). Brad is surnamed Zebatinsky (4), so he gave the gloves and received the jewelry box. By elimination, Max is Forbes. Nancy gave him a gift (see above), so she isn't Kublicek (8), so Jacob is Kublicek. By elimination, Nancy is Hong.

Alison Schumer gave a picture frame to Claudia.
Claudia Whittaker gave a keychain to Jacob.
Jacob Kublicek gave a jewelry box to Brad.
Brad Zebatinsky gave gloves to Nancy.
Nancy Hong gave sunglasses to Max.
Max Forbes gave a video game to Alison.

41 LOST IN TRANSLATION

The first person in line heard the message in English and the eighth person spoke it in English (intro). The third person in line spoke the message in French (4), so the fourth person heard it in French (intro). The sixth person in line heard the message in Navajo (7), so the fifth person spoke it in Navajo (intro). The language in which the fourth person spoke the message is the same as the language in which the fifth person heard it (intro). Thus, this language isn't Mandarin (2). Nor is it German or Italian, since that would make it impossible for those two languages to be paired together (8). Therefore the fourth person spoke the message in Spanish or Vietnamese. If it was Spanish, then the fourth person was either the aunt or the friend (9); if it was Vietnamese, then the fourth person was the school bus driver (6); therefore, the fourth person in line was the aunt, the friend, or the school bus driver. Thus, Cora's teacher was fifth in line (1). Since Cora's teacher didn't hear the message in Spanish (9), the fourth person in line didn't speak it in Spanish, so the school bus driver must have been fourth in line (see above), and spoke the message in Vietnamese to the teacher (6). Cora's friend and cousin were, in some order, third and sixth (3). By elimination, the people mentioned in clues 2 and 8 were, in some order, second and seventh in line. Cora's volleyball coach spoke the message in Mandarin (10), so she was first in line. Thus, the second person in line heard the message in Mandarin (intro), so this person spoke it in Spanish (2), and the third person heard it in Spanish (intro). The second and third people in line, then, were the aunt and friend (9), and since the friend was third or sixth (see above), the aunt was second, the friend was third, and the cousin was sixth (3). Cora's grandmother heard and spoke the message in German and Italian, in some order (8), so she was seventh in line, and by elimination the neighbor was eighth. The neighbor didn't hear the message in Italian (11), so he or she heard it in German. Thus, the grandmother spoke the message in German (intro) and heard it in Italian, and the sixth person in line spoke it in Italian (intro).

		heard	*spoke*
first	volleyball coach	English	Mandarin
second	aunt	Mandarin	Spanish
third	friend	Spanish	French
fourth	school bus driver	French	Vietnamese
fifth	teacher	Vietnamese	Navajo
sixth	cousin	Navajo	Italian
seventh	grandmother	Italian	German
eighth	neighbor	German	English

42 BENCHMARKS

Darius helped to fund the renovation of the tea garden (5). Ivan (who had a bench painted either green or white) helped to fund the improvement of either the basketball court or the playground (10). A man helped to fund the renovation of the local history museum (1), so by elimination this is Charles. The three women adopted: the blue bench, the bench dedicated to a grandmother, and the bench directly across from the bench whose adoption proceeds funded the game room (7). This accounts for all six people. The person who helped to fund the game room painted his or her bench either red or purple (13), so this person is the woman who dedicated her bench to her grandmother. The bench directly across from this, as mentioned in clue 7, is purple (2). Thus, the bench dedicated to the grandmother was red (13). This is bench #3 (3). The purple bench is directly across from this (see above), so this is bench #6. It was dedicated to an uncle (6). Of the six people mentioned in clue 4, the person who adopted bench #3 can only be Francine. Of the remaining five people mentioned in clue 4, the person who adopted bench #6 can only be the person who helped fund the theater. Ivan's bench isn't #1 or #5 (2). If his bench were #2, then bench #5 would be directly across from Ivan's bench, which is a contradiction (4). Thus, Ivan adopted bench #4, so Ivan is mentioned in clue 4 as the person who adopted a bench to honor his father. The yellow bench isn't #5 (4), nor is it directly across from Ivan's bench (4), so it isn't #1. Therefore, the yellow bench is #2. Charles didn't adopt this bench (1), so Darius did. Neither this bench nor the blue bench was dedicated to an aunt (9), so Charles dedicated a bench to his aunt. This isn't bench #1 (11), so it's bench #5. By elimination, bench #1 is the blue bench. It wasn't dedicated to a grandfather (11), so Darius dedicated bench #2 to his grandfather. By elimination, the woman who adopted bench #1 dedicated it to her mother. This woman isn't Anna (12), so Anna adopted bench #6. By elimination, Sophie adopted bench #1. She didn't help fund the playground (8), so she helped fund the basketball court. By elimination, Ivan helped fund the playground. He didn't paint his bench white (8), so Charles did. By elimination, Ivan painted his bench green.

#1	Sophie	blue	mother	basketball court
#2	Darius	yellow	grandfather	tea garden
#3	Francine	red	grandmother	game room
#4	Ivan	green	father	playground
#5	Charles	white	aunt	local history museum
#6	Anna	purple	uncle	theater

43 L'AMOUR, L'AMOUR

Either "Eternal Flame" or "Maybe Tomorrow" has a heroine named Paula (1). The novel whose heroine is Kat is set in either Marrakech or Tahiti (4). The novel about Trina is set in either Budapest or Singapore (9). Either "Maybe Tomorrow" or "Winds of Desire" tells Lyddie's story (12). Either Rafael or Scanlon falls for Zora (14). This accounts for the five novels. Either "Dare to Dream" or "Under the Spell" is set in Rio de Janeiro (2), so this is the novel about Zora. Rafael isn't in this novel (11), so Scanlon is. This isn't "Dare to Dream" (10), so it's "Under the Spell." "Dare to Dream" doesn't feature Kat (10), so it features Trina. "Winds of Desire" also doesn't feature Kat (10), so it features Lyddie. The plot of "Winds of Desire" doesn't involve a crisis in the world's gold market (10), so it involves a military coup (3). Of the novels in clue 10, Paula's can only be the one whose plot includes a crisis in the world's gold market. Neither Lyddie nor Paula, therefore, were the heroine in the novel set in Singapore that involves a bank robbery (5), so that is Trina's novel, "Dare to Dream." Zora's novel, "Under the Spell," which is set in Rio (see above), doesn't involve assassinations (11), so it involves a train derailment. By elimination, Kat's novel involves assassinations. That novel isn't "Maybe Tomorrow" (11), so "Maybe Tomorrow" is Paula's novel, and by elimination, Kat's novel is "Eternal Flame," set in Tahiti (7). Scanlon's novel involves a train derailment, so Aidan is the hero of the novel with the military coup (8), "Winds of Desire." Rafael isn't the hero of "Maybe Tomorrow" (11) or "Eternal Flame," which involves assassinations (11), so he's the hero of "Dare to Dream." "Maybe Tomorrow," whose heroine is Paula (see above), doesn't include Chase (13), so Chase is the hero of "Eternal Flame." By elimination, "Maybe Tomorrow" includes Hargrove. This novel isn't set in Marrakech (6), so it's set in Budapest. By elimination, "Winds of Desire" is set in Marrakech.

"Dare to Dream"	Trina & Rafael	Singapore	bank robbery
"Eternal Flame"	Kat & Chase	Tahiti	assassinations
"Maybe Tomorrow"	Paula & Hargrove	Budapest	gold crisis
"Under the Spell"	Zora & Scanlon	Rio	train derailment
"Winds of Desire"	Lyddie & Aidan	Marrakech	military coup

44 REUNION RECOLLECTIONS

Five of the six women are: Bethany, the woman who went to Wellesley, the woman who lived in Japan, the carpenter, and the graphic designer (8). The kindergarten teacher is either Alison or Kayley, and went to either Rutgers or San Diego State (12), and she lived in Brazil, India, or Spain (3), so she's the sixth woman. Samantha lived in either Denmark or Spain, and is either the decorative painter or the make-up artist (14), so she went to Wellesley. The restaurant manager didn't live in Japan (7), so she's Bethany. The woman who lived in Egypt isn't the graphic designer or the restaurant manager (2), or Samantha (14), or the kindergarten teacher (3), so she's the carpenter. Caroline didn't go to Egypt or Japan (11), and isn't the kindergarten teacher (12), so she's the graphic designer. Zoe is the decorative painter (5), so she lived in Japan. By elimination, Samantha is the make-up artist. She didn't live in Denmark (13), so she lived in Spain (14). She is surnamed Briggs (3). Caroline is surnamed Romo (1). She didn't live in Denmark (13), nor did the kindergarten teacher (3), so Bethany did. By elimination, Caroline Romo lived in either Brazil or India, so she went to the University of Virginia (3). The woman who went to Duke University isn't Bethany the restaurant manager (7); Zoe, who lived in Japan (7); or the kindergarten teacher (12). Thus, she's the woman who lived in Egypt. She isn't Ms. Torricelli (7), and neither is Bethany or Zoe (7), so the kindergarten teacher is Ms. Torricelli. She didn't live in India (10), so Caroline Romo did. By elimination, Ms. Torricelli lived in Brazil. She isn't Kayley (9), so Kayley is the carpenter. By elimination, Alison is Torricelli. She didn't go to San Diego State (4), so she went to Rutgers (12). Zoe didn't go to San Diego State (6), so she went to Harvard. By elimination, Bethany went to San Diego State. Neither Bethany nor Zoe is surnamed Chan (6), so Kayley is. Zoe isn't Ms. McAllister (5), so Bethany is McAllister. By elimination, Zoe is Ms. Wolfe.

Alison Torricelli	Rutgers	Brazil	kindergarten teacher
Bethany McAllister	San Diego	Denmark	restaurant manager
Caroline Romo	University of Virginia	India	graphic designer
Kayley Chan	Duke	Egypt	carpenter
Samantha Briggs	Wellesley	Spain	make-up artist
Zoe Wolfe	Harvard	Japan	decorative painter

45 CURTAINS FOR YOU

The dining room curtains are cotton or linen (2). The room with silk curtains has only one window, which is small (5). Andrea's living room has two large windows (10). The bedroom has corduroy curtains (12). The room with muslin curtains has one large window (15). The satin curtains are for either the kitchen or guest room (16). This accounts for all six rooms. The living room doesn't get linen curtains (6), so the dining room does. By elimination, the living room gets cotton curtains. These aren't taupe (6), so they're gold (3), and that room has 3 small windows (7). The guest room has 2 small windows (13) and 2 large ones (4), so it has satin curtains (see above). The bedroom has 3 large windows (6). The room with muslin curtains has 3 small windows (6). It also has 1 large window (see above), so it isn't the library (9), so the library has silk curtains. By elimination, the kitchen has muslin curtains. These aren't taupe (6), so they're white (11). Another room has 2 small windows and 1 large window (14), so this is the dining room. The room with blue curtains has no small windows (1), so this is the bedroom. The library has yellow curtains (8). The dining room has linen curtains (see above), which aren't taupe (6), so they're champagne. By elimination, the guest room has taupe curtains.

bedroom	blue	corduroy	0 small	3 large
dining room	champagne	linen	2 small	1 large
guest room	taupe	satin	2 small	2 large
kitchen	white	muslin	3 small	1 large
library	yellow	silk	1 small	0 large
living room	gold	cotton	3 small	2 large

46 WINE TASTING

The wine tasted third ranked 6th (3), and it was white (1). The Malbec ranked 2nd (12), and it wasn't one of the first four wines tasted (1). The 5th-ranked wine's label was either gold or tan (14). The Shiraz wasn't ranked 1st or 8th (6), or 2nd or 6th (see above). If the Shiraz had ranked 3rd, then the first wine tasted would've ranked 2nd (6), which is a contradiction. If the Shiraz had ranked 4th, then the wine with the blue label would've been ranked 5th (6), which is a contradiction. If the Shiraz had ranked 7th, then the first wine tasted would've ranked 6th (6), which is a contradiction. Therefore, the Shiraz ranked 5th, the first wine tasted ranked 4th, and the wine with the blue label ranked 6th (6). Thus, the wine with the blue label was tasted third (see above). The Viognier was tasted second and the wine with the maroon label was tasted first (11) and ranked 4th (see above), so the Cabernet Sauvignon ranked 3rd and the wine tasted fourth ranked 1st (16). Thus, the Viognier tasted second had either a silver or yellow label (2, 5) and the Pinot Grigio was tasted first (5), so it ranked 4th (see above). Therefore, the Sauvignon Blanc ranked 1st (13), so it was tasted fourth (see above). By elimination, the Chardonnay was tasted third (1), so it ranked 6th (see above). The wine tasted seventh ranked 8th (4), and since it was red (1), by elimination it was the Pinot Noir. Also by elimination, the Viognier that was tasted second (see above) was ranked 7th. The wine with the orange label must have ranked 8th (8), so this was the Pinot Noir that was tasted seventh (see above). That means the Viognier must be the lower-ranked of the two parting gifts, so its label is yellow (2). The wine tasted eighth was a parting gift (7), so it had a silver label. This is a red wine (1), but not the Cabernet Sauvignon ranked 3rd (15), nor the Shiraz (whose label is gold or tan), so it's the Malbec, ranked 2nd. Neither the Sauvignon Blanc nor the Cabernet Sauvignon has a tan label (10), so the Shiraz does. The wine with the gold label wasn't tasted fourth or sixth (9), so it was tasted fifth. The Shiraz with the tan label was tasted sixth. By elimination, the Cabernet Sauvignon was tasted fifth and the Sauvignon Blanc has the lavender label.

first	Pinot Grigio	maroon	4th-ranked
second	Viognier	yellow	7th-ranked
third	Chardonnay	blue	6th-ranked
fourth	Sauvignon Blanc	lavender	1st-ranked
fifth	Cabernet Sauvignon	gold	3rd-ranked
sixth	Shiraz	tan	5th-ranked
seventh	Pinot Noir	orange	8th-ranked
eighth	Malbec	silver	2nd-ranked

47 CLOSET CHRONICLES

The three girls are: the child Molly worked with on Tuesday, the 11-year-old, and the child who helped clean the hall closet (7). Jake is either 9, 10, or 12 (3). Ben helped either Monday or Wednesday (10). Cash helped clean either the bedroom or office closet (13). This accounts for the six children. The child who helped clean the laundry room closet isn't Jake or the 11-year-old (3), or the child who helped on Tuesday (14), so it was Ben. This happened on Wednesday and Katie helped on Monday (10, 14). Katie isn't 11 (1), so she helped clean the hall closet (7). The photo album was found on Tuesday (15), so the child who helped on Tuesday isn't 12 (11). Furthermore, the 12-year-old helped clean either the dining room or library closet (4), so the only child that can be the 12-year-old is Jake (see above), and Ben, who helped clean the laundry room closet, is 10 (3). Norah is 8 (5), so she is the girl who helped on Tuesday (7), and by elimination, Tonya is 11. Katie, who helped on Monday, is 9 (1). By elimination, Cash is 7. He didn't help clean the bedroom closet (6), so he helped clean the office closet (13), and this was on Thursday (2). Norah, who is 8, also didn't help clean the bedroom closet (6), nor did Jake, who is 12 (4), so Tonya did. Thus, Katie, who is 9, helped clean the closet where the bridal veil was found (6). Since this was on Monday (see above), the recipe book was found on Friday (9). The diploma was found on Saturday (10). By elimination, Jake and Tonya helped on Friday and Saturday in some order. Thus, Jake and Tonya helped find, in some order, the diploma and recipe book (see above). Cash, who is 7, didn't help clean the closet where the Christmas ornaments were found (11), so Ben did. By elimination, Cash helped clean the closet where the record collection was found. Thus, a girl helped clean out the dining room closet (12), so this is Norah. By elimination, Jake helped clean the library closet. This wasn't on Saturday (8), so this was on Friday, when the recipe book was found (see above). By elimination, Tonya helped on Saturday, when the diploma was found (see above).

Mon.	Katie	age 9	hall	bridal veil
Tue.	Norah	age 8	dining room	photo album
Wed.	Ben	age 10	laundry room	Christmas ornaments
Thu.	Cash	age 7	office	record collection
Fri.	Jake	age 12	library	recipe book
Sat.	Tonya	age 11	bedroom	high school diploma

48 CANDLE-MAKING AT CAMP

Jordy's candle, the candle shaped like a bunny, and the candle given to the piano teacher are, in some order, cobalt blue, navy blue, and sky blue (7). The gold candle was scented with either cinnamon or patchouli (2). The maroon candle was given to either the cousin or basketball coach (18). A girl made the olive green candle (20). This accounts for the six candles. Walker gave the candle he made to either his rabbi or his sister (4), so it was either the candle shaped like a bunny or the gold candle (see above). Ralph gave the candle he made to either his sister or his uncle (13), so it was also either the candle shaped like a bunny or the gold candle (see above). Therefore, these two boys made, in some order, the candle shaped like a bunny and the gold candle. A girl gave a candle to her basketball coach, but not the girl who made the olive green candle (20), so this candle was maroon (see above). The remaining girl gave a candle to her piano teacher, so this candle was shaped like an owl (20). The sky blue candle was shaped like either a pyramid or the Statue of Liberty (1), so Jordy made it. The child who gave a candle to his or her cousin made a candle shaped either like a bunny or a car (12). That's not the candle shaped like a bunny or the gold candle, which were given to two of the rabbi, sister, and uncle, nor is it the sky blue candle shaped like a pyramid or the Statue of Liberty, so it's the olive green candle and was shaped like a car.

Beyoncé's candle was shaped like either a hand or a pyramid (6), so it was maroon. Thus, Lauren's candle was olive green (3). By elimination, Kylie's candle was shaped like an owl, and it was scented with either cinnamon or vanilla (17). The navy blue candle was scented with either patchouli or sandalwood (15), so it was shaped like a bunny. By elimination, Kylie made the cobalt blue candle. It was scented with vanilla (5). A boy made the candle shaped like a hand (19), so it was gold. Beyoncé made the candle shaped like a pyramid (6). By elimination, Jordy made the candle shaped like the Statue of Liberty, and gave it to his rabbi (8). Walker gave his candle to his sister (4). By elimination, Ralph gave his candle to his uncle. We don't yet know whether Ralph made the navy blue or gold candle, but we know the navy blue candle is scented with patchouli or sandalwood, and the gold candle with cinnamon or patchouli. The candle given to Ralph's uncle wasn't scented with cinnamon or sandalwood (9), so it was scented with patchouli. A girl made the candle scented with maple (11), but not Lauren (16), so it was Beyoncé. Jordy didn't make the candle scented with lavender (14), so Lauren did. The hand-shaped candle scented with cinnamon was gold (10), so Walker made it. By elimination, Jordy made the candle scented with sandalwood, and Ralph made the navy blue candle shaped like a bunny.

Beyoncé	pyramid	maroon	maple	basketball coach
Jordy	Statue of Liberty	sky blue	sandalwood	rabbi
Kylie	owl	cobalt blue	vanilla	piano teacher
Lauren	car	olive green	lavender	cousin
Ralph	bunny	navy blue	patchouli	uncle
Walker	hand	gold	cinnamon	sister

49 EXOTIC PORTS OF CALL

Marion's six cruises were: The 2011 cruise, the cruise on the Orion, the cruise out of Marseilles, the nine-day cruise, the cruise where she met Tobias, and the April cruise (18). The cruise where she met Tobias was four days longer than the 2012 cruise and two days longer than the cruise from Curaçao; as shown above, the cruise where she met Tobias wasn't nine days long, so it lasted ten days, the cruise from Curaçao lasted eight days, and the 2012 cruise lasted six days (20). The cruise on the Sapphire was in 2011 (1). This cruise didn't last for nine or ten days (see above), so it was the eight-day cruise from Curaçao, and the cruise in February lasted for five days (16), which means the 2013 cruise took place in April (13). Thus, Marion's ten-day cruise where she met Tobias was in 2014 (4), which in turn means the May cruise was the eight-day cruise (8), which was the 2011 Sapphire cruise out of Curaçao. Her voyage on the Orion took place in June (2). The five-day cruise in February must have sailed from Marseilles (18). The six-day cruise in 2012 was on the Orion (18). By elimination, the seven-day cruise was in April 2013 (18). Her cruise from New York was in 2014 (10), so this was the ten-day cruise where she met Tobias. This wasn't in January (19), so by elimination it was in March and the nine-day cruise was in January. The Jasmine cruise lasted ten days (15), so it occurred in 2014. Marion met Tobias on this cruise (see above), so she met a woman on the five-day cruise out of Marseilles in February (5). Marion's friend from the Harmony is a man (12), so this cruise was in January (19). This was the nine-day cruise (see above), so she also met a man on the Empress (9), so this was in April 2013 on the seven-day cruise. By elimination, Marion sailed on the Albatross in February, so she met Hans on the January cruise on the Harmony (7). She met a man on the Empress in 2013 (see above), so by elimination this was Grigori. She sailed out of Singapore in 2012 (17), so this was the six-day trip. She met Clarissa on the five-day trip (3), which took place in February. The voyage out of Istanbul took place in January (11), so this was on the Harmony. By elimination, the Empress sailed from Bermuda in 2013. Marion met a man on the 2010 cruise (14), so this was Hans (see above). By elimination, she sailed on the Albatross in 2009 from Marseilles. Marion met Yolanda in 2011 (6), so this was on the Sapphire. By elimination, she met Shirley on the Orion in 2012.

2009	Albatross	Marseilles	five days	Clarissa	February
2010	Harmony	Istanbul	nine days	Hans	January
2011	Sapphire	Curaçao	eight days	Yolanda	May
2012	Orion	Singapore	six days	Shirley	June
2013	Empress	Bermuda	seven days	Grigori	April
2014	Jasmine	New York	ten days	Tobias	March

Zanaba sat directly between Nadia and the architect (9), so Zanaba is a woman, as is the person who sat on the other side of the architect (20). The architect isn't Eugene or Matthew (10), or Brian or Scott (16), so the architect is a woman. Thus, four women who sat consecutively were Nadia, Ms. Zanaba, the architect, and another woman. Because the four women sat consecutively, by elimination the four men also sat consecutively, so every pair of people seated directly across from each other are of opposite sexes. Thus, Nadia sat in seat #2 (2), so a man sat in seat #6, so he is Lindstrom (6). Matthew sat in seat #5 (17), so a woman sat in seat #1. Thus, Ms. Zanaba sat in seat #1, the architect in seat #8, and the remaining woman in seat #7, and men sat in seats #3 and #4. The person in seat #4 ordered pepperoni (4). Matthew didn't order pepperoni (10), so the person who sat in seat #3 ordered pepperoni (19). Eugene didn't order pepperoni (10), so he didn't sit in seat #3 or seat #4, so he sat in seat #6 and is surnamed Lindstrom. So far, five of the eight people mentioned in clue 10 have been accounted for, so Frobisher and Kendall are, in some order, the people who sat in seats #2 and #7. By elimination among the people in clue 10, Zanaba is the person mentioned here who ordered mushrooms. By elimination among the men, Brian and Scott sat, in some order, in seats #3 and #4. Neither of them is surnamed Duchovny, and neither is the architect (16), so Matthew is Duchovny. Iris is surnamed Walters (1), so she sat in seat #8. She ordered red peppers (6). The person who sat in seat #4 is the graphic artist, and he also ordered red peppers (15) in addition to the pepperoni we already know was ordered by the person in that seat. Scott ordered ham and onions (3), so he didn't sit in seat #4, so he sat in seat #3. By elimination among the men, Brian sat in seat #4. Iris Walters, who sat in seat #8, ordered artichokes (21) in addition to the red peppers we already know she ordered. She didn't order both chicken and tomatoes, so Matthew Duchovny did (11). Eugene Lindstrom, who sat in seat #6, is the security guard, and the woman who sat in seat #7 ordered tomatoes (7). This woman is mentioned in clue 16 as a person who ordered tomatoes, so she isn't surnamed Frobisher (16), and is therefore surnamed Kendall, while Nadia in seat #2 is surnamed Frobisher. Of the people as yet unaccounted for in clue 16, Zanaba must be the bookkeeper and Eugene Lindstrom ordered feta cheese. One person ordered black olives, green peppers, and sausage (13), so this is Nadia Frobisher. She can't also have ordered chicken, so Iris Walters did (20). Anita sat next to at least one person who ordered onions (18), so Anita can't be Zanaba, whose neighbor on one side ordered black olives, green peppers, and sausage, and whose neighbor on the other side ordered red peppers, artichokes, and chicken. Therefore, Anita is Kendall and Eugene Lindstrom ordered onions. By elimination, Lisa is Zanaba. The history teacher sat directly across from Lisa (2), so Matthew Duchovny is the history teacher. The merchandiser ordered artichokes (8), so this can only be Anita Kendall, who sat directly across from the violinist (4), which means Scott is the violinist. He isn't Granger (12), so he's Robertson. By elimination, Brian is Granger and Nadia Frobisher is the dentist. Eugene Lindstrom ordered mushrooms (22). Brian Granger ordered at least two items in common with Scott Robertson (12). We already know they have pepperoni in common; by elimination the other item is ham. Lisa Zanaba ordered feta cheese and sausage (14). Anita Kendall sat directly across from Scott Robertson (see above), so she didn't order green peppers (5), so Matthew Duchovny did. By elimination, Anita Kendall ordered black olives.

#1	Lisa Zanaba	bookkeeper	feta cheese, mushrooms, sausage
#2	Nadia Frobisher	dentist	black olives, green peppers, sausage
#3	Scott Robertson	violinist	ham, onions, pepperoni
#4	Brian Granger	graphic artist	ham, pepperoni, red peppers
#5	Matthew Duchovny	history teacher	chicken, green peppers, tomatoes
#6	Eugene Lindstrom	security guard	feta cheese, mushrooms, onions
#7	Anita Kendall	merchandiser	artichokes, black olives, tomatoes
#8	Iris Walters	architect	artichokes, chicken, red peppers